AUTOGENIC TRAINING

AUTOGENIC TRAINING

A Clinical Guide

WOLFGANG LINDEN, PhD

Foreword by Paul Lehrer, PhD

THE GUILFORD PRESS
New York   London

To Stefan
who still knows how to relax without a manual

© 1990 The Guilford Press
A Division of Guilford Publications, Inc.
72 Spring Street, New York, NY 10012

Printed in the United States of America

This book is printed on acid-free paper.

Last digit is print number: 9 8 7 6 5 4 3 2 1

Library of Congress Cataloging-in-Publication Data

Linden, Wolfgang, Dr.
    Autogenic training: a clinical guide / by Wolfgang Linden.
        p.   cm.
    Includes bibliographical references.
    Includes index.
    ISBN 0-89862-551-3 (cloth)   ISBN 0-89862-454-1 (pbk.)
    1. Autogenic training.   I. Title.
    [DNLM: 1. Autogenic Training—methods.   WM 415 L744a]
RC499.A8L55   1990
615.8'512—dc20
DNLM/DLC
for Library of Congress   90-13970
                                                              CIP

Foreword

It may come as a surprise to many English-speaking practitioners and users of various stress-management methods that autogenic training is probably the world's most widely used self-regulation therapy. Worldwide it is much better known and accepted than such stalwarts of American stress-reduction methodology as progressive muscle relaxation, biofeedback, and the "relaxation response." In German-speaking countries it is practiced by a large proportion of general medical practitioners as a component in treatment for psychosomatic disease. The technique also is widely practiced in Japan and in the Soviet Union, and, as Dr. Linden points out, a large proportion of the autogenic training literature is in the German, Japanese, and Russian languages. Most of this literature has never been translated into English and has remained inaccessible to individuals without fluency in these languages.

The method originally developed from Dr. Johannes Schultz's interests in hypnotic phenomena and is, essentially, a form of structured self-hypnosis. It adheres to an important principle of hypnotic trance induction: that is, that the hypnotist is best advised to suggest phenomena that the subject is certain to experience. This is often done by orchestrating the trance-induction situation to insure that particular phenomena will be experienced. Thus the stage for autogenic training is set by having the subject sit in a physically relaxing position and focus the mind away from the worries of the day and toward relaxing physical and mental images. This is done in a context that produces a commitment to achieving a calm and minimally goal-directed state. Then specific suggestions are given to sense the physical accompaniments of relaxation. How could one experience anything else?

In fact the method is sufficiently sophisticated to anticipate the fact that other feelings *will* occur, including some unpleasant ones. The emphasis in autogenic training is on repeating the formula in a state of passive concentration, rather than on experiencing the specifically suggested phenomena. If the specific sensations are not achieved immediately they will come later, the subject is assured. Even if the *opposite* of these are produced—sensations of anxiety pain, or discomfort—this eventuality is woven into the theory of the technique's effectiveness. It is, after all, known that various meditative processes loosen the bonds of mental inhibition and may release physical and/or mental sensations and images that have lost their saliency and/or usefulness and have been repressed. Old memories may be experienced. Suppressed sensations of pain from old injuries or operations may be perceived. Such is the case when higher mental processes are suspended and the body is allowed to seek its own level of equilibrium. Although particularly unpleasant "autogenic discharges" must be managed with clinical skill and sophistication, they are not to be avoided and are signs that the body's homeostatic process are working.

Indeed, one need not even experience relaxation for the effects of autogenic training to be positive. This notion fueled a long-standing public dispute between Schultz and progressive relaxation proponent Edmund Jacobson, who taught people to cultivate a state of "zero tension" in the skeletal muscles. Schultz and Luthe contended that such a condition was unnatural, while Jacobson argued that autogenic training did not produce relaxation. Perhaps both sides were right. But it is evident that the two techniques have quite different goals.

Schultz's work was introduced to the English-language reader by his collaborator, Wolfgang Luthe, who long practiced the method in Canada. For years Luthe's six-volume work on the subject, of which the last was published in 1970, was the only definitive English-language source of information on autogenic training. Although authoritative and exhaustive in its coverage of the world autogenic training literature to that time, this *magnum opus* has, in recent years, often not been read by practitioners of self-regulation therapies. Reasons for this neglect are probably the same as those proposed by Linden as the reasons for this present volume. Most importantly, the work is now dated. Considerable research has taken place since Luthe's series was published, and much more is known about effective and ineffective applications of the autogenic method. Also, as Linden points out, that series did not adequately distinguish between conclusions based on case observations and those emanating from controlled investigations. I can personally remember going through considerable difficulty to hunt down and translate some of the references used to back up various categorical statements, only to find that they were reports of almost casual observations. A third problem with the original work on autogenic training is the structure of the explicit theory of the technique. It is couched in terms that are no longer accepted by the psychological community. Having originated early in the twentieth century, its theory of emotion is a product of his time: that is, it is mechanical and "hydraulic." Much has been learned since then about both the brain and cognitive function. Despite its shortcomings, Luthe's work is truly a classic, and should be read by the serious autogenic training practitioner, although it no longer suffices. Hence the need for the present book.

Further evidence of the need for this book is the proliferation of published work on "autogenic training" in which the procedure bears little resemblance to the original method. Simply giving instruction to people to imagine various relaxing sensations is not the same as administering autogenic training, regardless of the effectiveness or ineffectiveness of these methods. Autogenic training involves an exact procedure. If not followed, the staunch autogenic training advocate might predict disastrous results. Whether the effects of these other methods are positive or negative, they certainly are not "autogenic training." Now therefore is the time to rearticulate the autogenic method.

Dr. Linden has done this definitively in the current volume. In my view it should become the standard modern work on autogenic training. Linden presents a step-by-step manual for doing the "real" autogenic training, while presenting a rationale that is consistent with modern understanding of the mind and body. He also has reviewed the voluminous literature on autogenic training and summarizes the effects of controlled research on the subject. I hope that researchers and practitioners alike will use this manual and follow it precisely. On the basis of my own experience with autogenic training and its various offshoots, I believe that this will improve clinical effectiveness. Such standardization unquestionably will also help to clarify the research literature.

PAUL M. LEHRER, PHD
Robert Wood Johnson Medical School
Piscataway, N.J.

Preface

That the phrase "autogenic training" would have to appear in the title to this volume was clear from its inception, but the decision to also call it "a clinical guide" took much longer and reflects the more subtle intentions behind writing this book. For many years I searched and failed to find a concise, single English-language source that students and practitioners could use for learning about the practice of autogenic training. At the same time, I noticed that stress management manuals describing its application had become more and more popular. Also, because I am a native German speaker I was aware of many scientific and popular publications about autogenic training that had appeared in German but had not been translated into English. Altogether, these observations provided the impetus for the book.

There were a number of explicit expectations for this endeavour. The book was to be reasonably short so that it could be published at a cost that would encourage students and practitioners to but it as a reference text for their library or as supplementary course reading. It was to have a *how-to* character that—as I knew because I teach in a clinical psychology program—would appeal to students who often feel they learn too much theory and not enough "hands-on stuff." Yet I also wanted to summarize the supporting scientific research with an emphasis on controlled, sound research designs. It was to be a real practitioner–scientist (in that order) book. How well it meets these expectations is for the reader to judge. I welcome any kind of feedback users may have once they have tried working with the text and autogenic training itself.

I am deeply indebted to those many individuals who have contributed their time and skill to this book. Wherever the book pleases most it was probably their doing, wherever it is found lacking I take full credit. First of all there are those who read and critically commented on various earlier drafts: David Crockett, Ph.D., James Frankish, Ph.D., Carol Herbert, M.D., Tess O'Brien, B.A., and Maureen Whittal, B.A. They represented a valuable mini-sample of potential readers: graduate students in the mental health disciplines, clinicians and clinical researchers. Their experience ranged from "never heard about autogenic training" to active clinical users with highly varied patient populations for many years.

Liz McCririck and Barbara Anderson patiently put up with my miserable word processing skills and made the seemingly endless modifications and improvements. Frances Wen helped gather the mass of background material from often obscure sources. The staff at Guilford (Sharon Panulla, Susan Marples, Anna Brackett, and Paula Wiech) deserve my gratitude for sharing my enthusiasm, for fine-tuning the manuscript, and for keeping me on track.

WOLFGANG LINDEN, PHD
Vancouver, B.C.

Contents

Part I
Introduction

✧ 1 ✧

What Does This Book Try to Achieve?

Autogenic training (AT) is not nearly as well known in North America as it deserves to be, given the amount of available supporting research, favorable clinical experience, and its widespread use in Europe and parts of Asia. A major reason for the relative lack of popularity of AT may be that much of the original and supporting literature is published in German, and so relatively few North American clinicians and scientists can draw on it in their literature searches. For this reason, much of the material covered in this book is explicitly based on the German-language scholarship.

The primary objectives of this book are to review and discuss the basic research supporting autogenic principles and the results of controlled therapy studies and to present a step-by-step training program permitting standardized teaching of AT. This standardized approach should facilitate the comparison of AT effects across different patients and outcome studies.

These two objectives are symbiotically linked. A strong research base, capable of inspiring clinicians to use this strategy, can only be derived from data obtained through the standardized application of these techniques. By the same token, a well-trained clinician is expected to abstain from using therapeutic procedures until they have been demonstrated to be useful. Therefore, it is hoped that the AT procedures laid out here will facilitate a standardization of clinical practices, and thereby allow for more reliable research outcome evaluations. I also hope that the documented AT treatment successes described in this volume will encourage clinicians to include AT in their standard repertoire of treatment techniques. Many questions inevitably arise when a new (or only superficially known) treatment technique is introduced:

- How can one define AT? What is the mechanism of action?
- How does it differ from or overlap with seemingly similar procedures?
- How does one learn or teach it?
- Can it serve as a universal treatment? Does it ever harm anybody?
- Can everybody learn and benefit from it equally?
- What are the acute effects of AT? Does it actually produce measurable changes?
- Does AT have lasting effects that make it appropriate as a clinical treatment?
- Is it useful even for people who are not addressing specific problems?

This catalogue of questions was used to structure this book. Thus, the origin of AT is described and its research history reviewed. Empirical justification is provided for the six formulas that characterize AT. A step-by-step teaching section is also included, and outcome data for a wide variety of problems are presented. To facilitate standardization, an additional outline of the suggested standard training approach is provided as an appendix for quick reference.

This book is intended to be a *how-to* text, but a word of caution needs to be added on the issue of who should teach AT. Traditional writers, such as Luthe (1963), consider AT to be a medical treatment that should be provided by physicians because of its possible physiological effects. Given the intensive training that psychologists and other physical and mental health care providers receive today, however, there appears little reason to be overly restrictive about who can competently teach AT as long as the following two conditions are met. (1) A thorough understanding of human physiology is necessary to understand the changes likely to be reported by trainees, and (2) based on my experience, it is necessary that only those professionals who have mastered AT themselves teach it to others. AT instructors need to have experienced autogenic sensations for them to be credible and understanding instructors.

✧ 2 ✧

What Is Autogenic Training?

It is tempting to simply define autogenic training (AT) as a form of relaxation therapy. But AT has also been described as "a psychophysiological self-control therapy" (Pikoff, 1984) and "a psychophysiologic form of psychotherapy which the patient carries out himself by using passive concentration upon certain combinations of psychophysiologically adapted stimuli" (Luthe, 1963). Although these latter two definitions may sound wordy, they underline what is unique about AT as a form of autonomic self-regulation therapy. Above all else, the emphasis is on "self-control" and "patient-administered," and it is for this reason that this book does not come with a cassette or record that the patient can (or should) take home. The term autogenic is derived from Greek and can aptly be defined as self-exercise or a type of self-induction therapy. The creator of AT, Johann Heinrich Schultz, was a firm believer in the self-healing powers of the body. Although Schultz's first steps toward the development of AT preceded Cannon and his proposition of the homeostatic model of physiological func-

6

tioning (Cannon, 1933), the homeostatic principle, and more recent formulations of biological self-regulation theory (Linden, 1988; Schwartz, 1977), were clearly in Schultz's mind when he conceptualized AT (Schultz, 1932). Although the most typical application of autogenic training is to reduce autonomic arousal (i.e., to serve as a relaxation technique), the AT rationale embraces the full homeostatic model.

What is the homeostatic model and what does it have to do with AT? Cannon proposed that the goal of physiological functioning is to maintain an inner state of stability or balance called homeostasis. Examples of attempts to achieve physiological balance include the sleep–wake and hunger–eating–satiation cycles. In such cases fluctuation and change are normal, but they occur in a rhythmic, balanced manner. Sleep serves to "recharge the batteries," and humans and animals wake up on their own when "the batteries are refilled." During the waking state energy is expended until fatigue and exhaustion set in. Sleep then follows naturally. This cycle repeats itself on a daily basis for the entire life span, and therefore represents a prime example of physiological self-regulation or homeostasis.

Another good example of the homeostatic principle is the interaction of sympathetic and parasympathetic activations within the autonomic nervous system. Because understanding the activity of the nervous system is crucial to understanding the rationale for AT, a brief introduction to the nervous system may be useful here. A major functional distinction is made between the central nervous system (consisting of the brain and the spinal cord) and the peripheral nervous system. The central nervous system is the command center of the body. It regulates and integrates other bodily functions and is also considered to be the center of conscious thought. The peripheral nervous system is commonly subdivided into the somatic nervous system (which connects with involuntary muscles and regulates the functioning of the inner or visceral organs. The autonomic nervous system does not require conscious, volitional regulation and can operate without input from the central nervous system (hence the term "autonomic"). The activity of the autonomic nervous system is often outside a person's awareness, and was long presumed also to be out of a person's control. This belief in the inaccessibility of autonomic functioning was abandoned after Miller's (1969) pioneering experiments paved the way for biofeedback, which represents a volitional attempt to condition visceral organ activity.

On the basis of this brief introduction to the nervous system we can now concentrate on the interplay between the sympathetic and the parasympathetic branches of the autonomic nervous system. The effect that sympathetic versus parasympathetic innervation has on the functioning of the visceral organs is best demonstrated in a graphic format (see Figure 1).

Sympathetic (activating) and parasympathetic (inhibiting) innervation operate jointly to control visceral functions based on the homeostatic principle. If homeostasis were perfectly maintained for all physiological functions at all times and there was no other input, then there would be no disease and possibly not even death. Reality of course tells us otherwise. Schwartz (1977) has pointed out that although the autonomic nervous system does not require conscious regulation, its functioning is still influenced by central nervous system activity, which facilitates the continuous somatic and visceral adjustments necessary to deal with changing environmental demands. However, it is now firmly believed that when homeostatic, autonomic functioning is continuously overridden by central nervous system input (for example, in a state of ongoing stress), self-regulation breaks down, and a pathway for stress, which could lead to psychophysiological dysfunctions like headache or high blood pressure, is created. A very useful model describing the effects of extended stress on health is Selye's General Adaptation Syndrome (1956). Under continued high levels of demand the body first becomes activated to meet the challenge and resists for some time, but ultimately becomes exhausted. This can lead to a variety of negative health consequences, such as excessive cardiovascular, electrocortical, and hormonal activation.

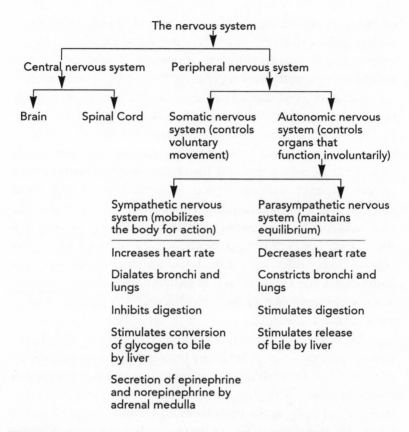

Figure 1. Breakdown of the human nervous system. The sympathetic and parasympathetic nervous system, though affecting the same organs, typically have opposing affects.

How is AT presumed to impact on nervous system activity? The objectives of AT are to reduce central nervous system (CNS) input (as typically seen during periods of stress) and to facilitate the return to self-regulation of visceral organ activity that the autonomic nervous system is presumed to govern. A successful AT outcome would be evident if electrocortical activity, an index of CNS activity, was operating at functional, alert levels, while cardiovascular and hormonal activity also operated within a functional range.

Because this theory is passive, permitting self-regulation

rather than provoking specific changes, AT should be useful in raising dysfunctionally low levels of autonomic function (for example, low blood pressure) to a normal, functional level. It should also permit down-regulation from an overaroused to a functional, relaxed state. The objective of AT is to permit self-regulation in either direction. Individuals gain the ability to induce deep relaxation or augment physiological activity through passive or self-hypnotic concentration. The patient (or trainee) is to concentrate on his or her bodily sensations in a passive manner without trying volitionally to bring about change. This clearly differentiates AT from other popular psychophysiological treatments such as biofeedback (Schwartz & Associates, 1987), where patients actively attempt to acquire control over autonomic functions, although it shares with biofeedback the assumption that bidirectional change (increase and/or decrease of a physiological activity) is possible and, in some instances, desirable.

AT is considered self-hypnotic. Yet, despite the shared term "hypnosis," the differences between self- and heterohypnosis need to be highlighted. In heterohypnosis the hypnotic trance is induced by another individual, such as a hypnotist, who will typically make relaxation and trance suggestions followed by suggestions for behavioral changes like stopping smoking, or feeling release from pain (Barber, 1984). The key difference is that AT, because of its self-hypnotic character, also promotes self-control and independence from a therapist.

Six standard formulas describing specific body sensations constitute the core ingredients of AT. The formulas are to be subvocally repeated by the patient. In addition, the patient is encouraged to develop personally meaningful images to accompany and enhance these formulas. An important feature that distinguishes AT from both muscular relaxation technique (Jacobson, 1938) and meditation (Wallace, 1970) is the targeting of specific bodily unctions within each of the six formulas. These formulas can also be modified to affect specific clinical target behaviors or organs.

Since AT shares many apparent similarities in rationale and technique with other methods, it needs to be empirically contrasted with these other biobehavioral treatment therapies, many of which, including biofeedback, hypnosis, muscular relaxation, and meditation, are currently in wide use (Woolfolk & Lehrer, 1984) The basic research supporting autogenic principles is discussed and contrasted with that of other biobehavioral treatment effects in Chapter 12. Another chapter (Chapter 13) is fully devoted to a review and discussion of comparative long-term clinical outcome studies involving these methods.

For easy comparison of different biobehavioral treatments a few characteristic features of each are provided in Table 1.

Table 1. Characteristics of Popular Biobehavioral Intervention Techniques

Techniques	Role of therapist	Vehicle of change
Autogenic training	Therapist instructs & guides, encourages self-control	Imagery of organ-specific changes.
Biofeedback	Therapist provides instrumentation, instruction, & guidance. Client partially controls the process.	Biological feedback and systematic behavioral/cognitive activity to acquire control.
Hypnosis	Therapist controls the process. Client is recipient.	Therapist suggestions.
Meditation	Therapist instructs & guides. Client controls process.	Repetition of meaningless syllable in imagery.
Progressive muscular	Therapist instructs & guides. Client follows instructions.	Systematic tensing and relaxing of specific muscle groups.

✧3✧

The History of Autogenic Training

Johann Heinrich Schultz, a German neurologist, is credited with the development and propagation of AT. During his medical training, first in dermatology and later in neurology, he became fascinated with hypnosis. This interest, however, was considered "unprofessional" by many of his peers. Initially, Schultz worked with hypnosis only after hours, when he was free of his regular clinic duties. The universal therapeutic approach of the time between the World Wars for all mental and psychosomatic problems was psychoanalysis. Schultz, however, rejected psychoanalysis as an effective treatment for psychosomatic disturbances. In a brief biography published in Schultz's honor, Schaefgen (1984) cites him as having said that "it is complete nonsense to shoot with psychoanalytic guns after symptom-sparrows". His breakthrough as the "father" of AT came after he had settled into the private practice of neurology and psychiatry at Berlin in 1924. There he could use and propagate AT without the constraints of clinic superiors who did not share his vision. The first presentation of his clinical experiences with

AT was in 1926 for his colleagues from the Medical Society. His first book followed six years later (Schultz, 1932). In all, he produced over 400 publications,- including numerous books that have been translated into six languages. By 1984 his groundbreaking book on AT had gone through 18 editions.

The development of AT as a novel technique appears to have been based on two sources: Schultz's own experiences with clinical hypnosis and Oskar Vogt's observations in brain research. Schultz noted that his hypnotized

Johann H. Shultz (1884-1970). Photo courtesty the International Society for Clinical and Experimental Hypnosis.

patients regularly reported two distinct sensations: "a strange heaviness especially in the limbs" and a similarly "strange sensation of warmth". He became convinced that hypnosis was not something that the hypnotist actively did to the patient, but rather was an experience that the patient permitted to happen. In order for the patient to enter a trance there had to be a "switch," a point of change. Provoking this switch and placing its control into the hands of the patient was what he wanted to achieve. Oskar Vogt's experiences further strengthened Schultz's belief that it was possible to trigger an autogenic state reliably. Vogt, a brain researcher, had reported to Schultz that his patients could produce the sensations of heaviness and warmth through mental concentration and thereby switch into a self-hypnotic trance. Therein the idea for the autogenic formulas was born. During the next years Schultz further developed his ideas concerning formulas that would reliably induce self-regulation and its accompanying sensations in various parts of the body. The publication of his 1932 book on AT was the culmination of his efforts to standardize the procedure.

AT did not become directly available to English-speaking researchers and clinicians until one of Schultz's followers, Wolfgang Luthe, a physician, emigrated to Canada and began publishing about AT in English. One important initial paper appeared in the *American Journal of Psychotherapy* (Luthe, 1963). This was later followed by a six-volume opus on AT that Luthe wrote partly with Schultz (1969–1970). Entitled *Autogenic Therapy, Volumes I–VI*, these texts provide the most detailed and comprehensive descriptions of all the facets of AT. Their exhaustive procedural, clinical, and research details represent a massive undertaking that only the most highly motivated reader can digest. The reader will find descriptions and success reports of AT for an enormous range of clinical problems. However, in the ultimate evaluation of AT's effectiveness no distinction is made between opinions, single case reports, and the preciously few controlled studies. The review of clinical outcomes in this book will therefore concentrate on controlled group studies only. By screening for the quality and the potential impact of previous publications on AT, the current book strives to provide summaries of this massive literature so that a fair balance between parsimony, persuasiveness, readability, and sufficient detail can be struck.

✧ 4 ✧

Status Quo of the Autogenic Training Literature

The perceived need for raising the profile of AT is based on systematic reviews of the literature. When I prepared a grant application for a therapy outcome study involving AT, I noticed a glaring discrepancy that has also been reported by two previous reviewers (Luthe, 1963; Pikoff, 1984). Although AT has been and continues to be very popular in Europe and parts of Asia, it appears to have few adherents in North America. Luthe (1963) noticed that of about 1,000 publications on AT only 1% were written in English. Pikoff (1984) similarly referred to 2,400 references in Luthe's 1970 series and found less than three dozen clinical reports on AT in English. All of this is striking because the procedure has been available for more than 50 years and is widely used in Europe. (By 1963 ten editions of the first German-language book on AT had appeared, along with translations into Spanish, Norwegian, French, and English.) The relative neglect of AT as a treatment

method in the English literature left me with two possibly in-
terrelated hypotheses. First, it could be that English-language
scientists simply do not read publications in other languages,
and therefore miss out on otherwise available information.
Second, the potential differences in how scientific information
is distributed in various countries or continents need to be considered: do English-speaking, particularly North American, scientists place different values on where and how information is
disseminated?

Having investigated these questions further, it appears
that both explanations hold some truth. It is typical in German publications to find many references to English publications (but rarely to works published in languages other than
these two). On the other hand, it is exceptional when an English publication cites anything that was not also published in
English. A scan of a number of randomly chosen journal
reprints confirmed this initial impression. In the German articles, three-fourths of the references were in English, and the
remaining were in German; in the English language articles
all of the references were in English. Similarly intriguing (and
in support of the second hypothesis) was an analysis of the
kinds of publications reflected in the more than 2,000 references of the six-volume series of Schultz and Luthe (1970) on
AT. A rough count revealed that 56% are journal publications,
13% are published conference proceedings, 14% refer to entire books, 13% refer to unpublished materials, and 4% are
book chapters. A breakdown of the languages in which these
works appeared identified 65% as German, 20% as French,
10% as English and the remaining 5% as Spanish, Portuguese,
Italian and Russian.

finally, one needs to raise the question of how much new
information is provided by these various types of publications.
Controlled therapy outcome studies with clinical populations
published in high-profile journals contribute the most to raising the profile of AT as a valuable treatment technique. How
many of the available publications on AT, however, represent

such widely read, valuable outcome studies? A literature search was initially executed in 1983 (and updated annually in preparation for this book) on the MEDLINE computer system concentrating on German- and English-language publications. The reason for including the German literature was that most of the earlier studies had been published in German. One hundred fifty-two references emerged with 90 titles in German and 62 in English. A breakdown of the English-language titles was most revealing: 18 out of 62 articles were on autogenic biofeedback (Fahrion, 1978), which is primarily biofeedback and hence misclassified under autogenics; five covered progressive muscular relaxation (again a misclassification); eight were not available in Canada's second largest library, nor could they be obtained via interlibrary loan; two dealt with hypnosis only (another misclassification); three were theoretical reviews; twelve represented anecdotal experiences, typically with single patients; nine reported AT effects on analog populations; and—finally—eight actually described autogenic effects in clinical populations. This pattern was equally apparent in the German publications.

What can one conclude from all of this? Although there are thousands of publications that deal with AT, very few represent the critical, controlled outcome studies that could firmly anchor its credibility as an effective treatment. Furthermore, some of these few, critical publications are not published in English. Against such a background, this book reviews the pertinent English- and German-language literature, identifies and critically discusses the empirical basis and the available therapy outcome data for AT, and provides a status quo report for clinicians and clinical researchers. My motivation to write this book was also spurred by my very positive personal experiences as a clinician frequently using AT, and by my belief that hidden in this mountain of already published pages is convincing evidence of the clinical effectiveness of this therapy.

A further objective of this book is to provide a standardized description of how to teach and practice AT with sufficient detail so that even the uninitiated reader (provided he or she has at least some clinical training) can use the book as a *how-to* manual. The need for more standardization of AT practices was underlined by Pikoff (1984) who concluded that North American researchers have taken great liberties with the original method, and have frequently shortened and/or modified it to such a degree that at the time of his review (1984) he felt that AT in its original form had never been properly applied and tested in North America.

Part II

A Clinical Manual

The manual section is adapted from Schultz's most recent description (1973) and is organized in the following manner: first, the physical settings for learning AT are described; second, the standard formulas and methods of introduction are laid out; third, possible problems and suggested solutions are highlighted; fourth, compliance enhancement and progress monitoring are discussed; and finally, upper-level AT (which has not been mentioned earlier) will be described. This will include the necessary training steps.

❖ 5 ❖

The Training Format and Setting

AT can be taught individually or in groups. The benefits and disadvantages of each are the same as for other forms of psychological therapy. Individual training is much more expensive, although such training can be adjusted to meet an individual's needs, financial as well as therapeutic, especially when AT is taught as part of complex intervention packages. The existence of a personalized therapeutic relationship may serve to enhance compliance and credibility. Group training is more cost-effective, but permits less individualized attention. On the other hand, a group has the potential to develop cohesion and serve as a support system for its members. This may have a positive impact on the therapy. My personal preference is to teach AT in groups of 8–12 participants, unless of course AT is integrated into an individualized treatment package requiring one-to-one therapy.

The ideal physical setting is one of comfort, with minimal possibility for disruptions. This should include a room temperature of 20°–22°C, a couch or exercise mattress (plus pillows) to stretch out on, and adjustable lighting. The exercises can only be effective when the person attempting to learn AT is completely focused on him- or herself. Any speech during the training impedes the basic principle of "autogenics." If the trainer talks too much, or plays a record or cassette, the trainee cannot really learn to exercise autogenically (independently). Rather, he or she will go through a light heterohypnosis. Such tranquility is therefore necessary for successful autogenic training.

In order to execute the training procedure, the trainee should be in a very comfortable sitting or, even better, lying position. A quiet and slightly darkened room is preferable. The entire body must be comfortable. Any discomfort may lead to muscle tension that will interfere with the progress of the exercises. It is advantageous to exercise in a lying position, with good support provided for the neck. The best support is often a rolled-up or fitted pillow. The arms should lie flat beside the body, slightly bent at the elbows, and the palms of the hands should be placed flat on the surface of the couch or mattress. The tips of the feet should be allowed to fall slightly to the outside (see Figure 2).

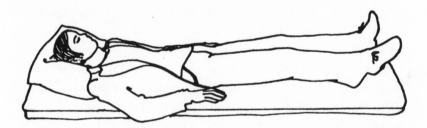

Figure 2. Ideal lying position for the practice of autogenic training. From *Ueberleben im Stress: Autogenes Training* (p. 33) by H. Lindemann, 1974, Muenchen, FRG: Verlagsgruppe Bertelsmann GmbH. Copyright 1974 by Verlagsgruppe Bertelsmann GmbH. Adapted by permission.

If this position is not possible or is impractical (for example, if the trainee wants to be able to practice in his or her office), a chair with a high back is best. The head should be supported and cushioned, and easily accessible side supports for the arms are preferable. The elbows should each be kept at nearly a right angle because in this position the stretch and bend muscles in the arm are in a balanced state. (The phenomenon of an "ideal" arm position is most apparent in individuals with arms paralyzed by stroke. In their case this arm position reflects a mechanical balance of the musculature involved.) The entire back and the back of the head should be fully supported, and the feet should rest close to each other with the soles flat on the ground. The knees should fall slightly to the outside, thereby helping to prevent tension in the thigh musculature. (Most people tend to close their knees while sitting. This position is often associated with unconscious muscular tension.)

When it is not possible for the trainee to either sit comfortably or lie down, a third position may be used for the exercise. One can sit on a bench or a chair without back support. In this position one lets the head sink into the torso and the arms hang at the sides. The head should be in a perfect vertical position over the spine. It is important that the trainee not bend forward. In this vertical position no muscular activity is necessary and no tension is created because the skeleton is held by the spine and its tendons. The arms can be moved loosely and can be supported by the widely spread thighs so that the forearms are supported by the thighs close to the elbow. The arms are again bent in the manner described above. The body now hangs on its own bone structure without any use of muscles (see also Figure 3).

These positions need to be mastered by the trainee before the exercises can begin. When this is accomplished one can begin with the first exercise. (It is best to use the lying down position, if possible, during the initial training sessions.) The

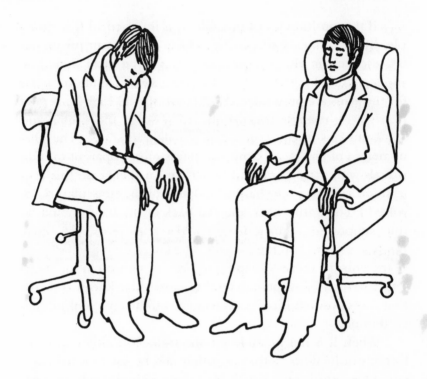

Figure 3. Ideal sitting positions for the practice of autogenic training. From *Ueberleben im Stress: Autogenes Training* (p. 32) by H. Lindemann, 1974, Muenchen, FRG: Verlagsgruppe Bertelsmann GmbH. Copyright 1974 by Verlagsgruppe Bertelsmann GmbH. Adapted by permission.

eyes should be closed because this facilitates the necessary concentration. The trainee should try to imagine the sensation suggested in the formula as fully as possible, without making any movement, trying to speak, or doing anything else. Ideas, images, and memories will necessarily develop in each individual, but these should not be fought off because the attempt to do so in itself could lead to tension. The training formulas should roll on continuously, as if on a tape.

When a trainee has effectively achieved an autogenic state (usually after about 10 minutes), he or she should not abruptly terminate the exercise by simply jumping up. Instead, trainees should slowly reactivate their muscular and breathing systems. This is achieved via a systematic "taking back" procedure. During "taking back" trainees are asked (over a 1-minute interval) to make a couple of fists and bend their arms inward (this prepares the muscles for action), then to breathe in deeply a few times and, finally, to open their eyes and sit up.

Before the rationale for the first formula is provided and the first AT practice begins, the trainer needs to ascertain whether all basic instructions and explanations have been given. The trainer is advised to keep a checklist so that each of the following items can be ticked off once it has been presented:

1. The overall rationale for AT and the steps in the learning process (see the outline in the Appendix for a suggested explanation)
2. The possible body positions during training
3. The "taking back" procedure
4. Realistic expectations for success
5. Possible unfamiliar sensations and feelings that can be anticipated
6. Details of the home practice assignments

Make sure that the trainees have fully understood all instructions and explanations and have had an opportunity to ask clarifying questions.

Each new formula is described in the same manner: a rationale and instructions are given and the exact wording and timing for each session are highlighted in a box. The description of each exercise is intentionally kept in nontechnical, everyday language so that AT trainers can borrow directly from this manual when they explain the rationales and steps to their trainees.

✧ 6 ✧

The Six Standard Formulas

Exercise 1: The Heaviness Experience (Muscular Relaxation)

In principle, one can approach AT from any one of a variety of different body areas and functions. (For example, one could begin with the breathing.) Autogenic training, however, begins with a focus on the musculature because this is most easily influenced by conscious efforts. In addition, experience has shown that a particular muscular relaxation can be achieved rapidly and notably through hypnosis and relaxation suggestions (Paul, 1969). Muscular relaxation is experienced as a heaviness of the extremities. Everyone is likely to have experienced this during nightly sleep. The extremities seem to "detach" themselves from the body.

Intentional concentration directed toward outside stimulation is associated with muscular tension. Looking, speaking, and reaching out are based on muscular movements. Attentional anticipation can also justifiably be called tension, since the muscles are already tensed in anticipation of movement. Even profound thinking can be seen as a muscular activity because in many people the forehead will fold while they are thinking. Each intention or imagining of a motion will result in increased tone of the musculature in the extremities.

It would be wrong at this time to attempt to use the entire body as an object of such training because the concentration would need to cover a field that is too large. The training should begin with one arm—a right-handed person starts with the right arm and a left-handed person with the left arm—and continue until the exercise effects have generalized to the other three limbs as well. If one arm has been trained for a reasonable period of time, the experience of heaviness during muscle relaxation will generalize to other body systems since all extremities and organs are accessed by the same nervous system. If from the outset of the training program the trainee uses one and occasionally the other arm without consistency, he or she will not obtain good results. arm first and to permit a generalized overflow of relaxation into the other extremities. Only those who strictly follow the instructions will develop real control and ease in the exercise procedures and will ultimately have success.

The complete set of instructions for exercise 1 (introduced in the first training session) is:

"Close your eyes, find a comfortable body position, and allow yourself to concentrate on what is going on inside of you. Nobody will disturb you. Just relax for a while." (*2 minutes*)

"Now concentrate on your dominant arm and repeat the formula six times, slowly. Use an image of heaviness that makes sense to you. The formula is: 'My right (left) arm is very heavy.' Use the formula six times." (*1 minute*)

"Now turn your attention away from the dominant arm
(cont.)

---

and say to yourself, just once: 'I am very quiet,' and enjoy feeling relaxed for a while." (*2 minutes*)

"Now concentrate on your dominant arm again and repeat
the formula six times, slowly. Use an image of heaviness that
makes sense to you. The formula is: 'My right (left) arm is very
heavy.' Use the formula six times." (*1 minute*)

"Now direct your attention away from the dominant arm
again and say to yourself, just once: 'I am very quiet,' and enjoy
feeling relaxed for a while." (*2 minutes*)

"I will soon ask you to take back, counting down from four
to one." (*Wait 15 seconds, then start counting down.*) "Four, make a
couple of fists in rapid succession to get the blood pumping
again." (*Wait 15 seconds.*) "Three, bend your arms inward a few
times." (*Wait 15 seconds.*) "Two, take a few deep breaths and fill
your lungs with air." (*Wait 15 seconds.*) "And one, open your
eyes, sit up, and you feel relaxed yet alert."

Total time: 9 minutes

Only if the relaxation is taken back in precisely the same manner each time can the trainee develop a reliable technique. AT
can only bear fruit when this technique is completely mastered. The individual also has to pay attention to the timing of
the exercises. During the first 7 to 14 days the training should
be repeated two times per day. In each training session one
can work a total of two times for about 1 minute on each formula. Following this, the sessions can be extended to 15–20
minutes as long as the subjective experience is pleasant. In the
beginning the individual exercises are often extended because
many trainees want to do them particularly well. This may
bring on many semiconscious tensions, however. Trainees will
realize that the experience of heaviness, instead of increasing,
will begin disappearing with continuous training if they try
too hard.

After 4 to 6 training days the feeling of heaviness in the trained arm will be more pronounced and will occur more rapidly. (This experience will usually begin to occur in other extremities at the same time as in the other arm.) When the experience of heaviness is quite pronounced, the formula can be changed to "arms heavy." Similarly, during taking back the terms can be changed to "bend arms," "breathe deep," and "open eyes." Experiencing heaviness in the legs does not necessitate a particular taking-back procedure since legs function more autonomically. Normally within 7 to 10 days the exercises have proceeded to a point where only a brief moment of inner concentration on the arms and legs can lead to a strong perception of heaviness. This signals the need to approach the second exercise.

Exercise 2: Experience of Warmth (Vascular Dilation)

Muscular exercises are something that the naive individual will find easy to do since muscular activity is typically considered to be a voluntary act. The idea that blood vessels may constrict or dilate through intentional effort usually seems more novel. However, it should be noted that all emotional activity tends to be associated with a change in blood flow (Linden, 1987) that may appear as flushing or paleness. The trainability of vessel changes in the hypnotic state is also well known. This second exercise, which aims at the warmth experience, affects the entire peripheral cardiovascular system. It affects the arteries (i.e., main blood vessels) as well as the capillaries in the organs, the venous blood flow, and the flow of blood through the skin and musculature. The distribution of blood in the vessels is regulated by the constriction and dilation that take place as a response to nervous system innervation. Its magnitude and direction are determined by one's physical activity, general state of arousal, and inhibition. Once the first exercise has been well trained and is rapidly inducible it can be extended by the inclusion of the second formula:

"My arm is very warm."

In a normal individual an inner, streaming, flowing sensation of warmth is noticed very rapidly, typically in the area of the elbow and the lower arm. Just as the heaviness associated with muscular relaxation can be monitored with electrophysiological devices, it is also possible to demonstrate the experience of warmth as an observable change in the living organism. The warmth radiation can be measured and has been determined to be a more than 1°C increase in body warmth and a 6–8°C increase in tissue warmth when the exercise "the arms warm" has been well trained. AT practice is to be executed with precision for a period of 1 or 2 weeks until the experience of warmth becomes more and more pervasive, first in the trained arm and then later in all four extremities. This experience of heaviness and warmth will also generalize to the entire body.

The standard training program of 8 weeks (see Appendix) suggests including one training session (typically the third) when no entirely new formula is trained. Rather, the heaviness and warmth formulas are combined and applied to both arms simultaneously. The blood vessel dilation and associative relaxation have a particularly tranquilizing and sleep inducing effect. It should also be mentioned here that training exercises directed at blood vessel dilation are not harmless since the changed distribution of blood influences the entire organism. This type of exercise should be instituted in healthy individuals only for whom no vascular risks are known to exist.

The complete set of instructions for adding formula 2 (typically introduced in the second training session) is:

"Close your eyes, find a comfortable body position, and allow yourself to concentrate on what is going on inside of you. Nobody will disturb you. Just relax for a while." *(2 minutes)*

"Now concentrate on your dominant arm and repeat the formula six times, slowly. Use an image of heaviness that makes sense to you. The formula is: 'My right (left) arm is very heavy.' Use the formula six times." *(1 minute)*

"Now turn your attention away from the dominant arm and say to yourself, just once: 'I am very quiet,' and enjoy feeling relaxed for a while." *(2 minutes)*

"Now concentrate on your dominant arm again and repeat the new formula ('my arm is very warm') six times, slowly. Use an image of warmth that makes sense to you. The formula is: 'My right (left) arm is very warm.' Use the formula six times." *(1 minute)*

"Now direct your attention away from the dominant arm again and say to yourself, just once: 'I am very quiet,' and enjoy feeling relaxed for a while." *(2 minutes)*

"I will soon ask you to take back, counting down from four to one." *(Wait 15 seconds, then start counting down.)* "Four, make a couple of fists in rapid succession to get the blood pumping again." *(Wait 15 seconds.)* "Three, bend your arms inward a few times." *(Wait 15 seconds.)* "Two, take a few deep breaths and fill your lungs with air." *(Wait 15 seconds.)* "And, one, open your eyes, sit up, and you feel; relaxed yet alert."

Total time: 9 minutes

When a new exercise step is added in autogenic training, as the experience of warmth has been added to the feeling of heaviness, the trainee should always concentrate initially on the already known exercises, and add the new exercise only for very brief periods (as has been described above in the heaviness exercise). Once heaviness and warmth in both arms can be rapidly and reliably achieved, the third exercise can be added. This typically occurs in the fourth weekly training session.

Exercise 3: The Regulation of the Heart

The heart is a very strong pumping muscle that works continuously with only extremely brief relaxation periods. The innervation of the heart, which accounts for the heart rhythm, is finely tuned by the nervous system. By learning the experience of warmth the trainee has already acquired the skill to influence a body system that was initially considered autonomous (the blood vessels). The relaxation of muscles was achieved by concentration on the experience of heaviness, and the dilation of blood vessels was achieved through the experience of warmth. A similar technique will be used in the next exercise.

How does one *feel* heart activity? An individual often becomes aware of the physical symptoms of his or her heart in times of strain, excitement, and fever, but normal heart activity is not obvious without prior training. Trainees need to be sensitized to this activity. Those who do not perceive their heart activity at the site of the heart can use their pulse for orientation. With further training they will learn to experience the activity of the heart itself.

If concentration on the pulse is not sufficient one can try to sensitize the trainee to heart activity in a more structured manner. This can be done by having the trainee lie flat on his or her back so that the right elbow is fully supported and lies at the same height as the chest. The right hand is to be placed in the heart area. The left arm position remains unchanged. The individual should then go into the usual state of heaviness, warmth, and quietness, and concentrate on any experiences in the chest where the hand is touching. The pressure of the hand functions as a directional indicator. After a few exercises most individuals become able to recognize heart activity, and with continuous repetition of the entire exercise ("heaviness–warmth–quietness") the experience becomes conscious:

> "My heartbeat is calm and strong."

The complete set of instructions for adding formula 3 (typically introduced in the fourth training session) is:

> "Close your eyes, find a comfortable body position, and allow yourself to concentrate on what is going on inside of you. Nobody will disturb you. Just relax for a while." *(2 minutes)*
>
> "Now concentrate on both arms and repeat the formula six times, slowly. Use an image of heaviness and warmth that makes sense to you. The formula is: 'My arms are very heavy and warm.' Use the formula six times." *(1 minute)*
>
> "Now turn your attention away from the arms and say to yourself, just once: 'I am very quiet,' and enjoy feeling relaxed for a while." *(2 minutes)*
>
> "Now concentrate on the beating of your heart, and repeat the formula ('My heartbeat is calm and strong.') six times, slowly. Use the formula six times." *(1 minute)*
>
> "Now direct your attention away from the heart and say to yourself, just once: 'I am very quiet,' and enjoy feeling relaxed for a while." *(2 minutes)*
>
> "I will soon ask you to take back, counting down from four to one." *(Wait 15 seconds, then start counting down.)* "Four, make a couple of fists in rapid succession to get the blood pumping again." *(Wait 15 seconds.)* "Three, bend your arms inward a few times." *(Wait 15 seconds.)* "Two, take a few deep breaths and fill your lungs with air." *(Wait 15 seconds.)* "And one, open your eyes, sit up, and you feel relaxed yet alert."
>
> Total time: 9 minutes

When the heart sensation has been learned (and in a sense has been "discovered"), the hand does not need to be placed any longer in the area of the heart. The exercise can then be continued in the usual position. During the exercises it should be highlighted that the intent of the exercise is not to slow down the heartbeat since this could cause damage. The emphasis of this exercise is on quiet and strong beats, not on a reduction of the heart frequency. Only under the supervision of a trained professional should an individual attempt to influence his or her pulse.

Exercise 4: Regulation of Breathing

Breathing is partially an intentional and partially an autonomous activity. In AT the muscular, vascular, and heart relaxation becomes immediately integrated with the rhythm of breathing, just as heaviness and warmth will automatically generalize from the trained arm to all of the other extremities. This generalization effect is typically observed. In the AT procedure, however, an intentional modification of breathing is undesired since an intentional change would be associated with tension through a reflex-type mechanism. Again, the trainee is to enter all the other exercise levels before the new, fourth formula is added:

> "It breathes me."

For many trainees it is tempting to try to achieve voluntary changes in breathing, or to make this procedure into a systematic breathing exercise as is known for example in Yoga. Intentional modification needs to be prevented in AT since breathing is supposed to function autonomously and in a self-regulatory manner without any active adjustment. In order to prevent such attempts at intentional change the passive-sounding phrase "It breathes me" is recommended. This statement should make it clear that relaxation and the regulation of breathing will come by themselves, and that the trainee is to give in to his or her own breathing rhythm just like a swimmer might become almost totally passive when floating on his back. When a trainee has made good progress with this exercise, which typically takes 7–10 days, the entire training period for steps 1–4 inclusive has now reached 5–6 weeks.

The complete set of instructions for adding formula 4 (typically introduced in the fifth training session) is:

"Close your eyes, find a comfortable body position, and allow yourself to concentrate on what is going on inside of you. Nobody will disturb you. Just relax for a while." (*2 minutes*)

"Now concentrate on both arms and repeat the formula six times, slowly. Use an image of heaviness and warmth that makes sense to you. The formula is: 'My arms are very heavy and warm. Use the formula six times." (*1 minute*)

"Now turn your attention away from the arms and say to yourself, just once: 'I am very quiet; and enjoy feeling relaxed for a while." (*2 minutes*)

"Now concentrate on the beating of your heart and repeat the formula ('My heartbeat is calm and strong.') six times, slowly." (*1 minute*)

"Now direct your attention away from the heart and say to yourself, just once: 'I am very quiet,' and enjoy feeling relaxed for a while." (*2 minutes*)

"Now concentrate on the rhythm of your breathing and repeat the formula ('It breathes me.') six times, slowly." (*1 minute*)

"Now direct your attention away from the breathing and say to yourself, just once: 'I am very quiet,' and enjoy feeling relaxed for a while." (*2 minutes*)

(cont.)

"I will soon ask you to take back, counting down from four to one." (*Wait 15 seconds, then start counting down.*) "Four, make a couple of fists in rapid succession to get the blood pumping again." (*Wait 15 seconds.*) "Three, bend your arms inward a few times." (*Wait 15 seconds.*) "Two, take a few deep breaths and fill your lungs with air." (*Wait 15 seconds.*) "And one, open your eyes, sit up, and you feel relaxed yet alert."

Total time: 12 minutes

Exercise 5: Regulation of Visceral Organs (Sun Rays)

Similar to the relaxation of the peripheral extremities, chest, and heart is the relaxation of visceral organs. For this the trainee imagines the area of the solar plexus, which is the most important nerve center of the inner organs. The image associated with this nerve center will be that of a sun from which warm rays will extend into other body areas. The solar plexus is found halfway between the navel and the lower end of the sternum in the upper body. The trainee now concentrates on this body site after formulas 1–4 have been fully trained:

"Warmth is radiating over my stomach."

This exercise also takes approximately 7-10 days to learn for normal individuals. This fifth exercise is added to the previous steps in the same manner as described above. An image of the breath streaming out of the body when the subject breathes out will help with this particular exercise.

The complete set of instructions for adding formula 5 (typically introduced in the sixth training session) is:

"Close your eyes, find a comfortable body position, and allow yourself to concentrate on what is going on inside of you. Nobody will disturb you. Just relax for a while." (*2 minutes*)

"Now concentrate on both arms and repeat the formula six times, slowly. Use an image of heaviness and warmth that makes sense to you. The formula is: 'My arms are very heavy and warm. Use the formula six times." (*1 minute*)

"Now turn your attention away from the arms and say to yourself, just once: 'I am very quiet; and enjoy feeling relaxed for a while." (*1 minute*)

"Now concentrate on the beating of your heart and repeat the formula ('My heartbeat is calm and strong.') six times, slowly." (*1 minute*)

"Now direct your attention away from the heart and say to yourself, just once: 'I am very quiet,' and enjoy feeling relaxed for a while." (*2 minutes*)

"Now concentrate on the rhythm of your breathing and repeat the formula ('It breathes me.') six times, slowly." (*1 minute*)

"Now direct your attention away from the breathing and say to yourself, just once: 'I am very quiet,' and enjoy feeling relaxed for a while." (*1 minute*)

"Now concentrate on your stomach area and repeat the formula ('Warmth is radiating over my stomach.') six times, slowly." (*1 minute*)

"Now direct your attention away from the stomach area and say to yourself, just once: 'I am very quiet,' and enjoy feeling relaxed for a while." (*2 minutes*)

"I will soon ask you to take back, counting down from four to one." (*Wait 15 seconds, then start counting down.*) "Four, make a couple of fists in rapid succession to get the blood pumping again." (*Wait 15 seconds.*) "Three, bend your arms inward a few times." (*Wait 15 seconds.*) "Two, take a few deep breaths and fill your lungs with air." (*Wait 15 seconds.*) "And one, open your eyes, sit up, and you feel relaxed yet alert."

Total time: 12 minutes

Exercise 6: Regulation of the Head

The well-known relaxing effect of a cool cloth on the forehead
forms the basis for this exercise. The trainee will enter stages
1–5 in the same careful and progressive manner described
above and will (initially only for a few seconds) proceed with
the first localized sensation. This is induced with the following
formula:

"The forehead is cool."

As warmth is associated with vasodilation, so the experience of freshness on the forehead will lead to a localized vasoconstriction and thereby to a lack of blood supply that in turn
accounts for the cooling effect. Because most walls are not entirely air tight there will usually be a slight movement of air in
any room. The cool forehead may therefore be sensed as a cool
breeze. Since all of the blood vessels of the organism are inter-
connected, localized vasoconstriction may possibly generalize
to other blood vessels in some individuals. This can be demonstrated by placing a finger in a basin of cold water. The entire
hand, and at times even the opposite hand as well, begin to
feel cool and pale. During AT the concentrative relaxation will
originate from the brain, a central organ that possesses the ca-
pability of changing the distribution of blood within the body.
This mechanism can occasionally lead to fainting or migraine
attacks during the "cool forehead" exercise. This exercise can
also be learned in approximately 7–10 days.

The complete set of instructions for adding formula 6
(typically introduced in the seventh training session) is:

"Close your eyes, find a comfortable body position, and
(cont.)

---

allow yourself to concentrate on what is going on inside of you. Nobody will disturb you. Just relax for a while." (*2 minutes*)

"Now concentrate on both arms and repeat the formula six times, slowly. Use an image of heaviness and warmth that makes sense to you. The formula is: 'My arms are very heavy and warm. Use the formula six times." (*1 minute*)

"Now turn your attention away from the arms and say to yourself, Just once: 'I am very quiet; and enjoy feeling relaxed for a while." (*1 minute*)

"Now concentrate on the beating of your heart and repeat the formula ('My heartbeat is calm and strong.') six times, slowly." (*1 minute*)

"Now direct your attention away from the heart and say to yourself, just once: 'I am very quiet,' and enjoy feeling relaxed for a while." (*1 minute*)

"Now concentrate on the rhythm of your breathing and repeat the formula ('It breathes me.') six times, slowly." (*1 minute*)

"Now direct your attention away from the breathing and say to yourself, just once: 'I am very quiet,' and enjoy feeling relaxed for a while." (*1 minute*)

"Now concentrate on your stomach area and repeat the formula ('Warmth is radiating over my stomach.') six times, slowly." (*1 minute*)

"Now direct your attention away from the stomach area and say to yourself, just once: 'I am very quiet,' and enjoy feeling relaxed for a while." (*1 minute*)

"Now concentrate on your forehead and repeat the formula ('The forehead is cool.') six times, slowly." (*1 minute*)

"Now direct your attention away from the forehead and say to yourself, just once: 'I am very quiet,' and enjoy feeling relaxed for a while." (*2 minutes*)

"I will soon ask you to take back, counting down from four to one." (*Wait 15 seconds, then start counting down.*) "Four, make

(cont.)

a couple of fists in rapid succession to get the blood pumping again." (*Wait 15 seconds.*) "Three, bend your arms inward a few times." (*Wait 15 seconds.*) "Two, take a few deep breaths and fill your lungs with air." (*Wait 15 seconds.*) "And one, open your eyes, sit up, and you feel relaxed yet alert."

Total time: 14 minutes

Summary of Exercise Steps

With these six formula-specific exercises AT has been described in its basic form. The entire set of exercises can now be summarized with the following formulas:

"Arm heavy"

"Arm warm"

"Both arms heavy and warm"

"Heartbeat calm and strong"

"It breathes me"

"Warmth radiating over my stomach"

"Forehead cool"

At the end "taking back": "make fists, arms bent inward; breathe; open eyes"

After about 8–10 weeks of training most individuals have acquired this set of exercises. Now the emphasis can be placed on ease in achieving the described sensations reliably and rapidly. Daily training for another 4–6 months will lead to more profound sensations. It is important to maintain the "taking back" procedure after each exercise (except when the trainee fell asleep during AT). The trainee will thereby acquire a readily available mechanism for switching from the tension of activity to deep relaxation and vice versa.

✧7✧

Possible Problems—Suggested Solutions

One of the objectives of this book is to provide a detailed description of the teaching and practice of AT so as to permit the standardized application of these techniques in clinical practice and thereby to facilitate the accumulation of valuable outcome data on AT in clinical research settings. However, anyone attempting to apply a standardized treatment via a manual like this will quickly find out that clinical reality and standardization are often incompatible. Trainees can lose motivation, undergo unpredictable and/or confusing training experiences, have medical or psychological problems that may interfere with learning and/or practicing AT, or have spouse/child/work obligations that may prevent regular practice. The list of potential problems goes on and on. Therefore good general, clinical skills are required to complement the training manual and to help to bring the training to a fruitful end. Nevertheless, some of these problems are well known to experienced teachers of AT and are either endemic to specific exercises or to the practice of relaxation at large. These typical problems, which can be anticipated, and some suggested solutions are presented in this chapter.

During the Heaviness Exercise

The heaviness exercise is the first in the AT program and is often the first experience with any kind of systematic relaxation for the patient. One can therefore expect, and in fact needs to anticipate, that the trainee will experience new, strange sensations. Many of these sensations are normal correlates of muscular and vascular relaxation, yet they may be new, puzzling, and perhaps even fear-arousing to the trainee. These include brief localized spasms, tingling, numbness, a pulling sensation, perceived swelling in the fingers, and/or a sense of detachment from a limb. Trainees may report none, one, or a few of these "odd sensations," and it is important to ask them about these at the end of the training session and to provide the requisite explanations. The patients should be assured that these are normal (even if not all of the trainees experience the same sensations) and that they will decrease in intensity and frequency with practice. It should also be pointed out that some cramping may be the result of "trying too hard," which often occurs when some trainees, who want to please the trainer, try to *make* the relaxation happen. These individuals need to be told—often repeatedly—that the purpose of AT is to *let* it happen passively. Muscle tension may simply be a sign of too much effort.

During the Warmth Exercise

Problems during the warmth exercise often manifest in one of two extremes. Some patients may actually report "burning," while others paradoxically note a cooling of the arm. These are usually initial problems that disappear with ongoing practice, but this does not mean that the trainees should necessarily be forced to endure unpleasant sensations for weeks on end. Instead, if, for example, acute burning is experienced, the trainee should rigorously take back. The unwanted sensation will usually disappear. The formula may be then changed somewhat to suggest "pleasantly warm," rather than "very warm."

During the Heart Exercise

Focusing on heart activity is novel for most trainees, and heart pulsations are reported from a variety of body sites: the chest itself of course, but also finger tips, feet, earlobes, temples, or the neck. Occasionally this sensation is described as anxiety-arousing (my heart is racing, or I feel heart pain). This has been especially true in patients with heart problems, or those with a latent fear of heart problems (Luthe, 1970a). While heart patients must be closely monitored by their physician, autogenic training should be recommended to these patients because of the beneficial long-term effects of AT for all kinds of cardiovascular problems. (See Chapter 13 for substantiation of this point.)

During the Breathing Exercise

Because breathing is particularly open to conscious manipulation it is very important that trainees do not actively try to change their breathing patterns. They are to observe a shift from thoracic to abdominal breathing and are to strive for regular breathing. To some, breathing appears to resemble "being lifted up and then lowered by a wave."

During the Sun Rays Exercise

The most frequent unwanted sensations during this exercise are rumbling, a feeling of pressure in the stomach, or crampy feelings. Typically these do not persist, but if the sensations are very unpleasant, rigorous taking back will eliminate them promptly. Many trainees become aware of hunger cues (if they have not eaten for a while), or they may notice some discomfort if they have had a particularly heavy meal prior to the training. Should the former be perceived as disturbing, it may be best to stop the exercise and eat a little before continuing. In the case of a full stomach, wait some time before trying again. In any case, practicing AT with great hunger pangs or a stuffed stomach is not a good idea.

During the Forehead Exercise

This sensation is the most difficult to achieve. An unsuccessful patient can be helped by the moisturizing of his or her forehead so that the freshness associated with condensation can enhance the cool sensation. Another modification can be made in the formula by adding, "Facial skin is relaxed and smooth." Occasionally trainees report dizziness, but this tends not to persist and disappears with rigorous taking back. Some trainees report having trouble falling asleep after the forehead exercise when they have used AT late in the evening as a sleep inducer. This can be solved by either skipping the forehead exercise at this time or by changing the formula to "Falling asleep is not important."

Outside Noise

There is no question that the learning of autogenics is facilitated by a quiet environment with minimal noise disruption.

However, it is frequently impossible to cut out all noise, nor can certain sudden noises (like a neighbor banging a door) be predicted or controlled. Furthermore, the positive effect of AT is probably best demonstrated when the trainee can continue relaxing even with a certain amount of noise in the background. When planning a session, however, the seeking of a noise-free environment should be the first step. Removing potential disruptions like the telephone, or alerting outsiders to an ongoing AT session by a "Do not disturb!" sign on the door are worthwhile preventive actions. Sudden unpreventable noises should simply be tolerated without undue attention. When setting up home practice assignments with trainees the therapist should not forget to suggest, as concretely as possible, how to arrange a noise-free, minimally interruptive, training environment. This may prevent the trainee from coming back 1 week later and reporting that it was impossible to practice AT because of such distractions.

Laughing and Talking

Especially at the beginning of their AT sessions the trainees may not be aware of the need to remain quiet, or they may find the instructions so strange that they laugh spontaneously. If the training occurs in a group this laughing may also be a reflection of an initial uneasiness with learning AT in front of strangers. In all of these cases the best strategy is to ignore the laughing and talking. If the trainer is consistent in providing the instructions and in not responding to chatter, laughter, or just spontaneous questions, then they will soon cease. The trainer should, however, also consider the possibility that he or she may have a truly theatrical or artificial style of interacting with the trainees that does indeed come across as funny and, ultimately, unprofessional.

An obvious exception to the rule of not attending to these vocalizations by the trainees during practice is the report of very disturbing, acute fears or unpleasant body sensations. In fact, it should be made clear at the outset that immediate reporting of such substantial discomfort is desired and necessary.

Falling Asleep

Many trainees will fall asleep during the practice of AT. This is clearly to be considered a sign of overall success, although it may not have been intended at that particular time. If the trainee falls asleep during a late evening, pre-sleep session this is perfectly okay. The question of taking back can be answered by suggesting that the trainee take back when he or she wakes up in the morning. Often AT sessions are held in the evening for trainees with daytime jobs or child- and housecare duties, and participants may naturally be tired by that time of day. If they do fall asleep during the training session, they of course need to be awakened. Experience has shown that clear instructions to take back in a noticeably loud voice will wake them up.

Itching, Coughing, Sneezing

Itching, coughing, and sneezing disrupt the practice of AT; however, they are so normal, frequent, and ultimately uncontrollable that they should simply be accepted. Relaxed trainees often become terribly aware of an itch and may feel it even more strongly because there are fewer sensory distractions. My advice to them is terribly simple. When it itches, scratch, and get back to your relaxation practice as soon as you can. Repressing the itch, the cough, or the sneeze cannot work for long. Doing so is also associated with muscular tension and thereby prevents the necessary focusing on the autogenic sensations. In my training groups I have noted that, especially with advanced trainees, nobody even twitches a muscle when another person sneezes, coughs, or makes a scratching noise.

These behaviors are not considered embarrassing and do not draw any particular attention.

Should sneezing, coughing, or itching be systemic to an illness like a major rash or cold, then it might be best to hold off AT practice because the disruption may be so strong and/or frequent that focusing on the AT formulas may become impossible.

Intrusive Thoughts

Because AT is a self-administered procedure requiring mental concentration and vivid imagery, competing thoughts may threaten the effectiveness of the relaxation formulas. Most frequent are thoughts of the harmless variety, which cause the mind simply to wander off. These can be triggered by an environmental noise or smell, or perhaps by reflection on the day's past activities or on plans the trainee might have for the session. In these instances the trainee should complete the thought, just as one would complete a sentence, and then focus again on the formula. This will become increasingly easy as the training progresses, and the suggested sensations become more rapidly and intensely apparent.

A considerable threat to relaxation, however, are more intrusive, obsessive kinds of thoughts that can be either related to outside problems or to the training session itself. Often during relaxation some unresolved problems that were pushed aside by day-to-day demands at work or home become very intrusive and vivid because strong distractions have been removed. Such problems could be related to ongoing marital conflicts, financial pressures, pending examinations, or performance pressures at work. In any case, not only can such intrusive thoughts jeopardize the effect of relaxation training, but there is actually a subgroup of relaxation trainees whose anxieties get aggravated during relaxation (Heide & Borkovec,

1983; see also Chapter 10). Simply telling the trainee to "stop thinking about these" is not likely to work. If such anxiety-producing thoughts do occur, they should be discussed with the trainer. Provisions should be made to deal with these concerns before or after the training session, or maybe even in individual therapy.

Another possibility is to teach the trainee a cognitive control technique (i.e., the trainee is to admit to him- or herself that there is a substantial problem that requires attention). However, this problem can be dealt with only after the AT session. When AT is being taught in a group, a trainee may experience these sorts of anxieties but feel inhibited to talk about them in front of others. The trainer can prepare for such occurrences by telling the group that at the end of the training session a few minutes will be allotted for anyone wanting to discuss more personal questions in a one-on-one manner. Clearly, in cases of intrusive, fear-provoking thoughts, it is obvious that a trained psychotherapist will be better equipped to deal with such problems than a layperson who is well versed in AT but inexperienced in mental health care otherwise.

Among the other intrusive thoughts that trainees may experience is sexual arousal. This can be triggered by thoughts about a person outside of the training situation or could be related to the therapist-patient relationship. Patients occasionally fall in love with therapists, and therapists are not always immune to the physical attractiveness and/or emotional needs of their patients. Elements of the training environment, including dim lights, a recumbent body position, the lack of outside disturbances, and the trainer's use of a soothing voice make sexual fantasies all the more likely. The advice to the trainee is similar to that given for intrusive, anxiety-provoking thoughts. They should be alerted to the likelihood of sexual arousal occurring during relaxation, and be informed that this is not unusual at all and therefore should not be met with particular concern.

Panicking over Loss of Control

Concern over loss of control is more justified during AT than during more structured forms of relaxation like Progressive Muscular Relaxation (Bernstein & Borkovec, 1973). Because AT is self-hypnosis that emphasizes letting go, it is often associated with the loss of control. This fear may get exaggerated because of the cloak of mystery that surrounds the term hypnosis. One step in the direction of preventing this sense of losing control is to emphasize that the procedure is applied by the trainees themselves, whenever and wherever they want. The trainer is no more than a teacher, who can be relied on for advice and information.

Still, some patients who are already anxious or overstressed may feel that they would go crazy if they ever let loose. One distinguishing feature of such individuals is their inability to relax, which is most noticeable in their continually tense muscles and is also apparent in their irregular or shallow thoracic breathing. The trainer should consider the possibility that these individuals may be on the verge of a true breakdown and in need of individual, psychiatric help. Many of them, however, are the very patients who should learn how to relax. They need AT the most but have the hardest time learning it. Consistent motivation and the pointing out of even the most minor progresses, while highlighting that this is a type of self-control training, may be sufficient for most. For others a more individualized, systematic desensitization to letting go may be required. Some of the basic elements of a relaxed posture, or even the dimming of the lights in the room, may be enough to trigger their loss-of-control panic. For such patients it is suggested that trainers begin with simple exercises involving noticing and verbalizing bodily symptoms and directing attention inward while the trainees sit upright with open eyes in a well-lit therapist's office. As a trainee's reluctance to relax wanes and somatic attention focus becomes possible, the therapist may begin to approach normal training procedures by first suggesting a reclined body position, and then adding dimmed lights. Finally, when all this can be done with subjective comfort, the suggestion to close the eyes can be made.

Autogenic Discharges

A phenomenon unique to AT is that of autogenic discharges, which are seen as sudden and unpredictable ways of "unloading" pent-up thoughts, sensory processes, and muscular activity (Luthe, 1970a). Although AT is presumed to have a gentle effect on autonomic self-regulation, the concept of autogenic discharges incorporates the idea that some of the self-regulation may occur through short bursts of CNS activity. Luthe (1970a) differentiates between discharges that are (1) reactive (that is, in response to acute provocation); (2) normally occurring spontaneous discharges, like motor discharges during pre-sleep stages; (3) originate from the brain and characterize pathology like epilepsy; and (4) discharges that may occur during sensory deprivation and during the practice of AT.

Unfortunately, this phenomenon is experienced with considerable variation in intensity and can take on many different forms. In consequence, one can debate whether trainees who do not report sudden discharges have them nevertheless but at a subliminal level (Luthe's position, 1970a) or whether in some patients they do not occur at all. Also, given that the discharges may take on different forms, one cannot rule out that the label "autogenic discharge" may simply cluster together a variety of phenomena with rather heterogeneous underlying neuro- or psychophysiological origins. One thing, however, is clear. Autogenic discharges when noticed by trainees are likely to be interpreted as bothersome and unwanted side effects of the procedure. Conversely, the traditional view in the AT literature is that autogenic discharges are necessary and considered to be signs of progress because they suggest a reduction in physiological/psychological inhibition. The important message for the AT instructor is to interpret these "weird" experiences of some trainees in this light and provide sensible, comforting explanations.

Data collected by Luthe (1970a) on two experimental groups may serve to explain the phenomenon further and illustrate the variety of possible autogenic discharge experiences. The two groups of subjects were all AT trainees who could be classified as either openly sexually active or as sexually deprived because of their particular life situations. The latter were clergy or otherwise prohibited by their adopted religions to be sexually active. The two groups were apparently similar in male/female proportion, age, clinical condition, and level of professional achievement. The experimental prediction was that the sexually deprived individuals would display more sexuality-related autogenic discharges than the controls, and indeed the results suggested just that. The sexually deprived group reported more itching, tingling, pain, and muscular twitches as well as more erections, vaginal spasms, and more sexual fantasies. The perceived sites of the most frequent sensory and motor discharges were thighs, lower abdomen, and genital regions.

The nature of the autogenic discharge and its explanation are unique to AT and direct comparisons with other self-regulation methods are difficult. It is my suspicion that some of the discharge phenomena also appear with other self-regulation strategies, but are simply considered to be negative side effects and are not attended to any further. Without a doubt, this phenomenon remains only vaguely understood and is in need of further investigation. Because autogenic discharges have not been reported with other relaxation techniques this also provides an additional clue for the uniqueness of AT.

❖ 8 ❖

Monitoring Progress and Maximizing Compliance

Compliance and the monitoring of a trainee's progress are intrinsically linked and are therefore discussed jointly in this section. Clearly, a trainee who does not see any progress despite twice-daily practice and weeks of training is going to lose the motivation to continue. In some ways this chapter could also be entitled "maximizing motivation" since motivation is the cornerstone of progress. Because progress is not immediately obvious a trainee with a strong motivation is more likely to succeed. It is therefore extremely important for the therapist to radiate confidence and a firmly anchored belief in the effectiveness of AT from the very beginning of training. A trainer who says, "I have heard that some people may actually benefit from AT as long as they practice every day for 3 months and never skip a practice session," will not instill much excitement or high initial motivation. Instead the therapist should give an optimistic but reasonable picture of the success to be expected: "I have trained *x* number of people or *x* number of groups and most patients have benefitted considerably. Even after *x* number of years I still practice it myself and have gotten all of my family members to learn it as well. Within the first two weeks you can expect the first training effects, which will only become stronger and easier to trigger as you keep on practicing." In all likelihood patients referred for AT have already heard good things about AT or the therapist (possibly both!) and so the therapist is riding on an initial wave of credibility. It is important to reinforce this, especially until the training effects themselves become apparent and take over as motivation enhancers. Even motivated patients, however, do not adhere perfectly to relaxation homework assignments. Taylor, Agras, Schneider, and Allen (1983) tested compliance with relaxation practice using a special tape recorder that displayed instructions but also unobtrusively monitored the number of times it was actually used. In this study 71% of the patients adhere to the instructions. Hoelscher, Lichstein, and Rosenthal (1986) similarly tested compliance with home practice instructions for relaxation and reported that compliance via self-report exceeded the actually monitored compliance by 91%, and that only 32% of the trainees averaged one practice per day. These results leave no doubt that poor compliance is a major problem and needs to be taken seriously. On the basis of other empirical findings on compliance (Haynes, Taylor, & Sackett, 1979) and this author's past experience with AT, a number of concrete steps are recommended for progress monitoring and compliance enhancement.

The Diary

Trainees should be asked to keep a diary where they tick off the pre-set, twice-daily practices, rate the depth of experienced sensations, and record any particular success or failure experiences. These should be brought to each session so that particular experiences can be easily remembered and discussed. At the same time this serves as a compliance check. Of course, they may still cheat and tick off a practice that they actually skipped, but this has not been a frequent occurrence in my experience, and in fact the diary serves as a useful reminder to trainees. A sample of an empty diary page like those used in my practice is found in the Appendix. This can easily be copied or detached for multiple uses. A copy of a completed diary page from the first week of training is displayed in Figure 4.

Trainees are to write at the end of the training session what their training goal for the week is. There are two spaces, one each for the twice-daily practices, to be ticked off after completion, and there is a rating of the perceived training success. Asking trainees to rate the intensity of their perceived sensations is geared to maximizing the self-fulfilling prophecy principle. When trainees rate each practice after being told that the sensation will get stronger and stronger, they are likely to expect and report steady improvement. This will become even more powerful when they see the progressively higher ratings they have achieved. There is also space left to record any unusual feelings that may have worried them or that they consider to be distinct early signs of training success. The diary is of course very useful for the review of the past week's training experiences and should be addressed at the beginning of every therapy session. For maximum convenience and compliance, as well as to facilitate standardization, I actually supply all trainees with a preprinted, spiral bound diary that has a page for every training week. This prevents uneven record keeping and eliminates the excuse of "I could not find an appropriate booklet for a diary."

Timing of the Home Practice

Compliance on the taking of medications (Haynes, Taylor, & Sackett, 1979) has revealed that taking medications at prede-

Training week:____/____ From:__Aug 9____ To:__Aug 16__
Training goal for this week: _"right arm very heavy "_

Please tick off (✔) each exercise after you did it and use the following scale
to evaluate each time whether or not you reached this week's goal.

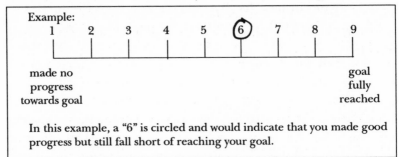

Example:
| 1 | 2 | 3 | 4 | 5 | ⑥ | 7 | 8 | 9 |

made no   goal
progress   fully
towards goal   reached

In this example, a "6" is circled and would indicate that you made good
progress but still fall short of reaching your goal.

Day 1	Excercise I:_✓_	Rating:_2_	(Fill in appropriate number.)
	Excercies II:_✓_	Rating:_2_	
Day 2	Excercise I:_✓_	Rating:_3_	
	Excercise II:_✓_	Rating:_4_	
Day 3	Excercise I:_✓_	Rating:_3_	
	Excercise II:_✓_	Rating:_3_	
Day 4	Excercise I:_✓_	Rating:_4_	
	Excercise II:_✓_	Rating:_4_	
Day 5	Excercise I:_✓_	Rating:_4_	
	Excercies II:____	Rating:____	
Day 6	Excercise I:_✓_	Rating:_4_	
	Excercise II:_✓_	Rating:_5_	
Day 7	Excercise I:_✓_	Rating:_5_	
	Excercise II:_✓_	Rating:_5_	

Figure 4. A sample diary page used by the author to document autogenic homework assignments.

termined times of the day, coupled with other already existing
routines, is an important vehicle for enhancing compliance. In
the same vein, I ask my trainees to think about and commit to
practice times in the first training session. I would rather deal
with their scheduling difficulties before they start practicing
than find out one week later that they did not practice at all be-

cause they could not find the time. When I say "predetermined" times I do not mean 6:47 p.m. every day. Rather, I mean fixed in the sense of "every night after I have finished watching the evening news" or "when I am in bed before falling asleep." AT practice must become a routine, requiring no thinking or planning effort, or else it is much too vulnerable to daily mood fluctuations or outside disturbances.

Need for Frequent Practice

AT trainees may find the rule of twice-daily practice for two months (or more) overly compulsive, and when faced with other demands on their time, may be tempted to cut back on the time allotted for practicing. My recommendation is to be understanding if one or two practices a week are skipped, but to continue to urge trainees to stick to the rule. This is more likely to occur if trainees clearly understand the reason for this rule. In the first session it should be emphasized that relaxation is a skill that requires practice. One could compare AT practice with learning to throw a baseball or learning the backhand in tennis—any and all of these skills require a great deal of practice.

Dropout

Although AT is popular, patients drop out for a number of reasons: they move away, there is too much competition for their time, the training effects are too slow in coming, or for a variety of other reasons. Even the most experienced therapist will have to face dropout and noncompletion rates of 20%–25% in AT. If the dropout rates are noticeably higher, then the therapist should question his or her ability to motivate patients. Lack of trainer enthusiasm, poor communication skills, poor session planning—any of these could be the culprit. I have also seen—although rarely—that some groups, for no apparent reason, never develop cohesion, or that occasionally a member is considered obnoxious by the others, which causes them to stay away.

Highlight Success

Finally, nothing breeds success like success, as the old saying goes. The therapist can use this principle by regularly asking the trainees whether they have tried autogenics in acute stress situations (like exam anticipation or before a confrontation with a superior). If so, he or she can highlight their success stories.

Trainees can also be asked regularly whether they have noticed any generalizations of training effects, such as improvement in the ability to fall asleep or to relax after a hard day of work, or a reduction in occasional tension headaches. Hearing in a group learning format that someone else has benefited from AT can serve as an extra motivator. The trainer should frequently praise such learners, not only for their apparently positive outcomes, but also for regular attendance to the training sessions and for keeping up with the home practice.

Especially during the first training sessions, when subjective effects are weak at best, the trainees may be very skeptical about the effectiveness of AT. At this time the instructor can use biological feedback to demonstrate physiological changes. Heart rate and blood pressure changes during AT practice can be monitored and "fed back" with user-friendly devices like digitized heart rate or blood pressure monitors. (These are commercially available for $100 or less.) The motor inactivity associated with relaxation practice, coupled with a rapid adaptation to a repeated measurement situation (Linden & Frankish, 1988), almost guarantee a measurable decrease in cardiovascular activity indices under these conditions. Although the researcher is aware that the explanation for this phenomenon is complex and not exclusively attributable to AT, the trainee will nevertheless be impressed and will likely attribute the observable changes to the AT practice. Such simple feedback may have a considerable booster effect on compliance and motivation.

✧ 9 ✧

Upper Level Autogenic Training

Upper level AT is made up of meditative exercises that can be used as extensions of the six basic formulas. Less is known about these exercises than about the six standardized formulas, and references to them are found in only a very few English-language publications (Davis, Robbins Eshelman, & McKay, 1982; Luthe, 1970a). A comparison of various sources reveals frequent differences in procedure, but there is a common body of formulas and themes that is used for these meditative exercises. They are, however, clearly less standardized than the six basic exercises. Below, a core program is described that has appeared in much the same format in a variety of different publications on AT (Davis et al., 1982; Krapf, 1984; Lindemann, 1974). It should be noted here that no therapy outcome study on upper level AT has been published yet.

The basic requirement for the upper level AT exercises is the mastery of the six basic formulas. Only those trainees who can promptly—that is, within one minute of concentration—produce an autogenic state are perceived to be ready for the upper level exercises. The training standard is a 7-week program with weekly sessions and a new topic each week. Each exercise is to last 10–20 minutes. This length has also been reported to be subjectively pleasant. The topics for each meditative exercise begin with color images and proceed through object visualization, affectively neutral abstract terms, perceptions of others, and imagery with symbolic value, such as visions of a "bridge," "my next step," or "a door to be opened." This order of topics is to reflect a flow toward increasing abstraction and increasingly more idiosyncratic, affectively loaded subjects, and is designed to develop the ability to visualize, and then to present images that possess high levels of symbolism and can serve as triggers for affective experience and discharges. The lines between biological self-regulation training, meditation, and psychotherapy become blurred with upper level AT. The objective of this therapy is to go beyond mere somatic sensations to access material of psychodynamic importance. In consequence, it is not possible to see how upper level AT could be responsibly guided by someone who lacks thorough training in psychodynamically oriented therapy. In fact, it would be frivolous and ethically questionable to do so because of the high likelihood of previously suppressed or repressed psychodynamic conflict coming to the fore.

Outlined below are instructions for a standard 7-week program:

First Session

The trainee is to begin this exercise (and all later ones) by assuming his or her favorite body position for AT practice, and quickly running through the six standard exercises. Then, with eyes closed, the trainee uses a typical self-hypnotic induction procedure—that is, the eyes are directed inward and upward as if looking into the center of the forehead. Patients with myopia may be advised to concentrate on the tip of the nose

instead. The basic formulas for all seven sessions are the same
(specifics are inserted as the central part of the exercises).

Quiet—Heavy—Warm

Heart and breathing calm and regular

Warmth radiating over stomach

Forehead pleasantly cool

Relaxation deepening

In front of my inner eye an image develops (use 3–5 times)

The image becomes more pronounced (use 2 times)

The image is very clear in front of me (use 2 times)

Taking back is also executed in the same manner for all
exercises.

The images are gradually fading.

The images are nearly faded.

The images are gone.

I count to six, at six, I feel very quiet, fresh and well.

One: my legs are light.

Two: my arms are light.

Three and four: Heart and breathing normal.

Five: Forehead has normal temperature.

Six: Arms bent in, breathing deeply, and open eyes.

Specific to the first session is the experience of color visualization. The trainee is to imagine seeing one color cover the
entire visual field. He or she is encouraged to try different col-

ors to ascertain which is easiest to visualize and which feels subjectively best. Trainees are also encouraged to play with the image, to let it fade and get more intense, to project frames into it and move these around, and to fill the frames with other colors and move them through the unicolor field. The exercise is meant to strengthen visualization ability and to generate a practice phase for learning to form, modify, and generally control mental images. During this and all later sessions the therapist serves as a facilitator who makes occasional suggestions. Ideally there should be minimal interaction after the initial instruction until the experience is discussed at the end of the training session.

Second Session

The second session is devoted to the visualization of concrete objects, such as pieces of fruit. The apple is a particularly popular choice, possibly because of its archaic symbolism in the Bible. The trainees should be encouraged to draw many details into their images and dwell on these for blocks of time.

Third Session

The third session moves on to the imagery of abstract concepts like movement, relaxation, or happiness. For happiness, for example, it is useful to think of the face of a happy person in a fairy tale or a movie. Opposing concepts, such as immobility and movement, or quiet and restlessness, can also be used in an alternating manner.

Fourth Session

Now, an actual person is introduced as a mental image. Preferably this is an individual with whom interpersonal difficulties exist. If this is too hard at the beginning, the image of a more neutral, but reasonably well-known person, such as a letter carrier or store clerk, may be used. The imaging of a disliked person, or of someone toward whom the trainee has ambivalent feelings, is likely to trigger vivid images and spontaneous insights that may be novel to the trainee. At this stage the presence and help of a trained psychotherapist is particularly opportune.

Fifth Session

The trainee is to visualize a bridge in as much detail as possible. The bridge image is chosen because of its symbolic content as a connector and/or dividing object. It can be understood as a symbol for interpersonal communication.

Sixth Session

Visualization of walking or running is the content of session six. The symbolism here is to be seen in the extent to which trainees feel free to move, to take large or small steps, and to be able to choose their direction or path.

Seventh Session

In this session the visualization of a door is chosen as a symbol for resistance and rediscovery of hidden emotions and images. Whether or not this door can be opened, the number and type of locks, and the anticipation of what is to be found behind it, are the protective themes underlying the visualization. Krapf (1984) reported an interesting case where a patient initially felt locked into a box as a child, and felt greatly relieved when she could finally imagine opening the lid, stepping out of the box, and even sitting on it.

Concluding Comments

Because these upper level exercises may trigger unpleasant psychodynamic themes, caution is in order. Trainees should quickly and rigorously take back when the images became too fear-arousing and threatening. Trainers need to monitor the experience carefully and be prepared to provide interpretation, guidance, and continued support if difficult psychological material emerges that suggests underlying, unresolved conflict. The upper level exercises clearly require integration into a supportive psychotherapy framework.

❖ 10 ❖

Matching Patient and Technique

When therapeutic techniques are shown to be effective for a given problem, this conclusion is typically based on comparisons of the group means of treated patients against their pretraining levels, against waiting-list, or against some other treatment controls. Hidden in such mean change comparisons is a considerable variability in treatment response, such that some patients benefit whereas others do not change or even get worse (Jacobson, Follette, & Revenstorf, 1984; see also Chapter 13). A clinician treating individual patients may, of course, not be satisfied knowing that a statistically significant mean change occurred in a treated group. Instead, the practitioner may want to attend to each individual's progress. Therefore, it is of great importance for practitioners using AT to be aware of what kind of patient can learn and benefit from this treatment and to know in advance whether AT is indeed the best method of treatment for a given patient.

The question of AT suitability given certain patient characteristics is addressed in this chapter, whereas the question of using the most powerful therapy technique for a specific problem will be addressed in the chapters that follow.

Can Anyone Learn Autogenic Training?

There is little doubt, either in the literature or in my experience, that the mechanics of AT can be taught to a wide variety of individuals. Yet, some caveats are in order. Adults of all ages and many children have learned AT, but children below school age lack the discipline and attention span necessary to master AT. Depending on the child's maturity, intelligence, and imaginative abilities, the lowest age at which AT can be taught effectively is somewhere between 6 and 10 years of age. Retarded individuals and those with acute central nervous system disorders or uncontrolled psychoses are likely to be unable to process and follow the instructions. Thus, with relatively few exceptions, AT can be learned by nearly everyone.

Will Everyone Benefit from Autogenic Training

Although there are few individuals who are unable to learn autogenic principles, there are also people who learn AT but may not necessarily show any clinical benefits. The practitioner has to consider the possibility that AT is not the treatment of choice for a given person. Four lines of research contribute valuable information to this discussion. The first is research on relaxation-induced anxiety (Heide & Borkovec, 1984). The second attempts to subdivide individuals based on the way they experience anxiety and then seeks optimal relaxation technique/personality matches for certain population subgroups (Schwartz, Davidson, & Goleman, 1978). The third pertinent area of research attempts predictions of relaxation training success by considering differences in initial resting levels and interindividual differences in response to the first training sessions (Vinck, Arickx, & Hongenaert, 1987). And finally, personality factors as predictors of success were specifically targeted (Badura, 1977).

The concept of relaxation-induced anxiety was propagated by Heide and Borkovec (1983) who observed that a surprisingly large number of trainees in Progressive Muscular Relaxation (PMR) became paradoxically anxious as they relaxed, given that relaxation training is conceived to serve as an anxiety reducer. These authors noted that trainees with high pre-training levels of generalized anxiety were most likely to become anxious when trying to relax. Although no similar, systematic studies of this type could be found for AT, Heide and Borkovec's work (1983, 1984) is of importance to AT because of the similarities in PMR and AT rationale and the associated relaxation outcomes. The existence of similar increases in anxiety is supported by anecdotal reports of rising discomfort during AT (Luthe, 1970a; and my own clinical experience). Furthermore, it appears that different types of relaxation training vary in terms of the likelihood of triggering enhanced anxiety in trainees. Heide and Borkovec (1983) solicited chronically anxious subjects and offered PMR or meditation. They noted that 30% of PMR-trained patients became more anxious during relaxation practice, whereas 54% of meditation-trained patients became more anxious. This observation is of interest because the greater incidence of anxiety induction during meditation was attributed to the less externally structured nature of meditation (relative to PMR). AT is also less structured (i.e., less closely controlled by the therapist) than PMR and may therefore possess a greater propensity to trigger relaxation-induced anxiety.

Heide and Borkovec (1983) offer a number of potential explanations for the paradox of increased anxiety during relaxation. The first explanation is that during relaxation a shift toward greater parasympathetic dominance occurs, which results in peripheral vasodilation and feelings of warmth and heaviness (formulas 1 and 2 in AT) (Budzynski, Stoyva & Pfeffer, 1980). The unfamiliarity with parasympathetic activity sensations may be particularly disturbing to chronically tense or anxious individuals. Also, relaxation frequently brings about unfamiliar spontaneous muscular skeletal events like myoclonic jerks, spasms, twitches, or restlessness. These experiences are referred to as "autogenic discharges" by Luthe (1970a). Another explanation centers around the notion of "fear of loss of control." Chronically anxious individuals may have learned to control their anxieties in the past by never letting go. They typically work in a compulsive, rigid manner and cannot permit themselves to relax (Martin, 1951). In a similar vein, Raimy (1975) has reported that 20–30% of college students surveyed have, at one time or another, experienced a fear of going crazy, which of course represents an extreme case of loss of control. These data suggest a relatively high prevalence of the "fear of loss of control," even in seemingly well-adjusted populations.

A relatively simple suggestion that may work for some of the anxious, overcontrolling patients is for them to conceive of relaxation as something they actively control, something that they can switch on or off at will. Also, I have frequently told my trainees that the ones who have the hardest time learning to relax are by definition the ones who need to learn it the most. The most important take-home message from this research is that relaxation-induced anxiety is not at all infrequent. It needs to be anticipated and actively dealt with. Complete disregard may be harmful to some patients and (unnecessarily) increase dropout rates and/or the variability of treatment responses.

The second line of research on matching patient characteristics to the choice of relaxation procedure was originated by Schwartz, Davidson, and Goleman (1978). Schwartz and his collaborators initially proposed that attempts at autonomic self-regulation involved distinct cognitive, somatic, and attentional processes, and furthermore posited that because people differ in their predispositions and perceptions of these processes, optimal treatment should acknowledge interindividual differences and should represent a tight match of therapy rationale, type of problem, and patient characteristics. In order to identify relevant subgroups of people, Schwartz and his coworkers developed a 14-item Cognitive–Somatic Anxiety Questionnaire that permits the identification of patients who experience anxiety primarily as either somatic symptoms (i.e., perspiration, shortness of breath, heart racing, etc.) or as cognitive symptoms (worrying, mental preoccupation, etc.).

A first test of this specificity hypothesis was undertaken by studying treatment responses to physical exercise relative to meditation on the somatic and cognitive components of anxiety. As predicted, subjects who exercised showed greater reduction in somatic anxiety while subjects who meditated showed greater decreases in cognitive anxiety. Norton and Johnson (1983) extended these findings with snake phobics who received either muscular relaxation or meditation, and who had a priori been classified as predominantly cognitively or somatically anxious. Muscular relaxation was better for somatic anxiety reduction and meditation was superior for cognitive anxiety reduction. Lehrer, Woolfolk, Rooney, McCann, and Covington (1983) further contributed to this literature by comparing patients undergoing muscular relaxation and meditation to a wait-list control. Although they reported more similarities than differences in outcome for the two active treatments, specificity was apparent in that meditation produced greater cardiac-orienting responses to stressful stimuli, greater absorption in a challenging task, and better motivation. Muscular relaxation, in contrast, produced greater decreases in forearm EMG responsiveness to stressful stimulation and an overall stronger therapeutic effect. Norton, Rhodes, Hauch, and Kaprowy (1985) followed up on the earlier studies and replicated Schwartz et al.'s (1978), Heide and Borkovec's (1983), and their own earlier findings (Norton & Johnson, 1983). The best treatment responses (defined as change in heart rate and subjective improvement) were observed for meditation in those subjects with high cognitive anxiety and the ability to absorb (i.e., openness to new experiences), and for muscular relaxation in subjects with low cognitive anxiety and little openness to new experience. Mismatches (i.e., meditation for low cognitive anxiety or muscular relaxation for high cognitive anxiety) were associated with relatively worse outcomes. These findings suggest that patient characteristics such as predominant anxiety experience can predict differential relaxation treatment outcomes and deserve consideration in individual treatment plans involving relaxation therapy. Unfortunately, the replicated findings in this research domain involve only meditation, exercise, and muscular relaxation. Therefore, it is not clear how AT outcome may be affected by individual predispositions to cognitive or somatic anxiety experience or specific reductions in cognitive versus somatic anxiety symptoms. My opinion is that AT is to be placed between meditation and muscular relaxation insofar as therapist control and involvement of imagination are concerned. Whether or not this implies that both cognitive and somatic anxiety are equally treatable with AT remains to be determined.

The third line of research deals with pretreatment differences between individuals. Vinck et al. (1987) attempted to predict blood pressure treatment responses in normotensives who learned either Progressive Muscular Relaxation (Jacobson, 1938) or AT. Training was provided weekly for 6 weeks. Relaxation effects were measured for within-session change during the first treatment session, for overall change in resting values from the first to the last treatment session, and for within-session change during the last treatment session. While overall differential effects for muscular relaxation relative to AT were reported, Vinck et al. (1987) did replicate Jacob, Kraemer, and Agras' (1977) findings that higher initial blood pressure levels predicted the greatest reduction with relaxation training. In addition, these researchers found that trainees with the least change during the first training session of either AT or muscular relaxation therapy were the ones who

showed the greatest reductions during the last training sessions. Attempts to predict blood pressure treatment response
via personality indices were unsuccessful.

Vinck et al. (1987) may have failed to identify personality
factors as predictors of relaxation (and implicitly AT) success
because their subjects were healthy individuals who reflected a
narrow range of associated personality features. No such range
restriction was apparent in Badura's work (1977). He related
Minnesota Multiphasic Personality Inventory (MMPI) profiles
to AT outcomes in 200 patients with neurotic, functional, and
psychosomatic symptomatologies. Badura's patients were subdivided into successes and failures on the basis of the reported
ability to achieve formula-specific autogenic sensations. Patients
in the "failure" group were characterized by a particular MMPI
profile with relative elevations on the hypochondriasis, depression, hysteria, and social introversion subscales. This profile is
also called the neurotic triad. Discriminant function analysis indicated that, using this distinct MMPI profile, 80% of the suc-
cess/failure incidences in AT could be correctly classified.

A number of conclusions and suggestions on the question
of "Can everyone benefit?" now appear justified. There is little
doubt that patients with elevated baselines on an autonomic
index (for example, blood pressure) profit more from AT (or
other relaxation therapies) than do those with lower baselines.
Similarly, those patients showing the least initial response to
treatment show greater improvement over time than those
with strong early responses (Vinck et al., 1987). Also, clinical
elevations on depression, introversion, hypochondriasis, and
hysteria scales predict poor AT outcome. Such individuals may
be better served by another form of psychotherapy. Evidence
for a specificity theory of somatic/cognitive anxiety expres-
sion, and the need for a suitable relaxation method to counter
this anxiety, is available but is not very strong and requires further clarification. It also remains unclear how AT fits into the
distinction between the cognitively based and somatically oriented relaxation therapies. To me it appears that AT contains

a good balance of both cognitive and somatic characteristics
and might therefore be equally suitable to very different patient groups. This opinion is as yet unsubstantiated and is certainly open to empirical testing.

⟡ 11 ⟡

AT Applications to Specific Problems: Modifying Formulas and Using AT in Multicomponent Therapy Packages

This chapter and the one following on controlled therapy outcome involving AT are designed to guide AT practitioners in their clinical decision making. The range of possible AT applications as documented by Luthe and Schultz (1969a,b) is vast. As yet, however, most descriptions of AT applications represent only clinical anecdotes, single case studies, and uncontrolled group research. The more practical, clinical approach taken in this chapter is of greatest value to the clinician who needs to make therapy plans on a case-by-case basis and who may have to make important clinical decisions even in the absence of an established research base. Descriptions of AT modifications made to suit specific case needs and of integrations of an AT component into multicomponent packages are to be found below.

The range of previous applications can be described best by repeating the application listings from the Luthe and Schultz (1969a,b) series. In each instance AT was applied to at least a single case, and often to multiple cases or groups. This list includes patients with Parkinson's disease; multiple sclerosis; tremors; tics; facial spasms; blepharospasm; spasmodic torticollis; neuralgia; phantom limb pain; narcolepsy; brain injury; epilepsy; cerebral palsy; manic–depressive illness; schizophrenia; paranoia; anxiety; dissociative disorder; conversion disorder; phobia; obsessive–compulsive behavior; hypochondriasis; schizoid, compulsive, and sociopathic personality disorder; sexual deviation; addiction (smoking, alcoholism, and illegal drugs); enuresis; masturbation; somnambulism; writer's block; stuttering; sleep disorders; auditory hypersensitivity; and pain reactions, as well as individuals seeking improved performance in education, sports and industry. (The above are listed as psychotherapy applications, both clinical and nonclinical.) The medical applications include disorders of deglutition; dyspepsia; peptic ulcer; biliary disorders; ulcerative colitis; irritable colon; constipation; food allergy; anorexia nervosa; obesity; sinus bradycardia, tachycardia, and arrhythmia; extrasystoles; auricular fibrillation; paroxysmal tachycardia; heart block; angina pectoris; myocardial infarction; cardiac neurosis; left mammary pain; blood pressure control; disorders of peripheral circulation (like Raynaud's disease); hemorrhoids; blushing; tension and migraine headache; bronchial asthma; pulmonary tuberculosis; diabetes mellitus; thyroid dysfunctions; lipid metabolism disorders; tetany; arthritis; nonarticular rheumatism; low back pain; hemophilia; disorders of micturition; sexual dysfunctions; gynecologic disorders; pregnancy complications and labor pain; skin disorders; blindness; dental pain; and preparation for surgery.

Clearly this is an exhaustive catalogue of possible and tried applications covering just about every disorder—whether psychiatric, psychosomatic, or somatic in nature—that can be mediated by nervous system activity. For the sake of brevity the topic of AT can be modified to suit specific needs. Samples of therapy packages involving an AT component will then be described, and finally, outcome data will be presented, but only when this is based on controlled studies.

Modifications of AT Formulas to Suit Specific Needs

Modifications of the standard formulas are typically of three types: (1) a reduced number of formulas are taught, typically the heaviness and warmth formulas; (2) the standard set is taught but one specific formula is left out; or (3) the standard formulas are taught and an additional, problem-specific formula is created and appended.

Teaching abbreviated AT would make sense if its effectiveness had been proven to be comparable to that of the long version, and if time considerations are crucial to a particular patient. Unfortunately, no such comparisons are available, although some abbreviated applications of AT have been found to produce therapeutic benefits. (See the following chapter for details.)

The need for the elimination of a certain formula from the standard set is often the result of an unanticipated difficulty, such as that certain formulas trigger negative associations, images, and/or memories for a particular trainee. This has been addressed already in Chapter 10. Another possibility is that of a rationale/application mismatch. For instance, a cardiac neurosis patient may, at least initially, be hypersensitive to all cardiac sensations, and therefore elimination of the "heart beats calm and strong" formula is advisable. These decisions require clinical, on the spot judgments. Excessive standardization and prescriptions based on a manual like this one may be inappropriate.

A particularly appealing modification for many therapists and their patients is that of a person- or disorder-specific additional formula. Lindemann (1974) has provided a rich fund of specific application formulas from which a subset is selected for demonstration here. With respect to formula additions (also called intentional formulas), there are really no limits for adapting formulas to idiosyncratic preferences in imagery or word choices, or to descriptions of desirable target behaviors.

Desirable characteristics of effective, intentional formulas are brevity, a pleasant rhyme or rhythm, and a positive choice of words. They should also be clearly relevant to the trainee, and a good match to his or her personality. Guidance for creating formulas with these characteristics can be drawn from Erickson and Rossi's (1979) book on hypnotherapy. The following are some examples of intentional formulas for specific problems:

"First work, then pleasure" to help against procrastination.
"I am happy, relaxed, and free of hunger" to accompany a weight reduction program.
"I sleep deeply, relaxed, and restful" for insomnia problems.
"I am calm and relaxed, my cheeks stay cool" to reduce blushing.
"I am completely relaxed and free, my stomach and bowels are working steadily and smoothly" to help relieve gastrointestinal complaints.
"I am totally quiet and in peace; my joints are moving freely and without discomfort; they feel warm" to diminish arthritis pain.

Autogenic Training in a Multicomponent Treatment Package

In clinical reality patients often present multiple complaints and/or the therapist discovers during an individual assessment that a given problem is likely caused or exacerbated by a multiplicity of factors. This in turn calls for a program of therapy with multiple components. While multicomponent therapy is the norm in everyday clinical work and is associated with better clinical outcomes than single component therapies (Shapiro & Shapiro, 1982), there are an infinite number of such treatment combinations possible. Thus, extensive and comparative outcome testing for each possible combination is not feasible. Clinical judgment, good training, and experience need to complement a therapist's awareness of research findings in order to judge the appropriateness of a treatment package for a given patient. The best packages tend to be those with strong, individually tailored rationales, and with components that were demonstrated to be efficacious when tested alone. Because of the infinite number of possible combinations of treatment techniques, only four treatment packages—one each for enuresis, asthma, stress management, and migraine—involving AT are highlighted here as samples. These were chosen because they reflect diversity and because they are perceived to be grounded in strong rationales.

Enuresis

Koldewy and Wegschneider (1963) have described a training program for enuresis that has achieved good clinical success in cases involving hundreds of children. The children are instructed in the standard AT formulas (time pressure limits the training to the heaviness and warmth formulas), and an intentional, enuresis-specific formula is appended. The intentional formula is directed at developing a mental clock so that children can wake up at will. The children are taught that the best solution to their problem is to learn self-control rather than to be constantly awakened by the parents during the night. It is explained that waking up on their own is more pleasant, and that being awakened during the deepest phase of sleep can thus be avoided. The "mental clock," so they are told, controls their sleep and can wake them up for use of the bathroom.

The intentional formula is worded as follows: "At 10 PM I will wake up on my own. I will get up and use the bathroom, return to bed and continue sleeping." The ability to read a clock and to understand the concept of time is of course a prerequisite, thus making this method available to children from about the age of 8 onwards. In addition, all progress is monitored and recorded in a "success diary" that permits contingent reinforcement on the next day. Both the improvement in the problem behavior and the successful waking-up procedure are recorded and reinforced. In a sample of 705 treated children, the authors reported a 31% rate of complete elimination of enuresis, and while 16% showed no change, considerable improvement was made by the remaining 53%. Using more recently developed concepts, the success can be explained as a result of a strengthening of the children's self-efficacy perceptions (Bandura, 1977), as well as of behavioral principles of reinforcement achieved through self-monitoring and therapist reinforcement (cf. O'Leary & Wilson, 1987).

Asthma

A detailed and promising, two-pronged strategy for asthma interventions involving AT has been described by Spiess et al. (1988; see also Chapter 13). The intervention itself is laid out here in a session-by-session format.

Because of the biological basis for asthma and the need to provide medication as a primary (or supplemental) therapy, this approach requires the expertise of a physician, preferably a pneumologist, and is ideally executed with a multidisciplinary team composed of specialists in both internal medicine/pneumology and psychotherapy. The treatment has an informational component, which is provided for groups of 15 patients in eight 90-minute sessions over an 8-week period. AT is later added as a complementary treatment in an additional, once weekly, 7-week program. Details about the informational component are listed session by session.

Session 1: Group members learn that asthma is a common problem and that they are not alone. The chronicity of the disorder is described, as well as the possible dependence on medication and the resulting feelings of lack-of-control and helplessness. patients are also made aware that knowledge of available treatment options can help to reinstate a sense of personal control.

Session 2: Patients receive formal instruction in the anatomical and physiological bases of asthma (at their level of understanding). They begin to understand how respiration is influenced by muscle spasms, excess secretions, infections, and environmental irritants. They also learn about functional measurement, the need to objectively monitor lung function, and that subjective experiences of breathing difficulties do not always reflect actual physiological activity.

Session 3: Patients learn about asthma medications, classes of drugs, differentiations between prophylactic and acute drug interventions, side effects, the possibilities and limitations of self-controlled drug intake, and get problem-solving training concerning when to consult their physician.

Session 4: Behavioral prescriptions for coughing, inhalation, physical therapy, and dealing with bronchial symptoms are provided. Patients learn when and why standard drug dosages need to be decreased.

Session 5: Appropriate behavioral responses during physical exercise and holiday times are discussed. Patients learn about types, prevalence, and behavioral responses to environmental allergens.

Sessions 6 and 7: Emotional responses to the illness are discussed. The practitioners learn about the patients' idiosyncratic illness models (and correct them where necessary), and opportunities are provided for patients to ventilate their dissatisfaction with the health care system. Fears centering around the chronic nature of the illness and around suffering from severe, possibly life threatening attacks are frequently brought up.

Session 8: The therapists explore whether or not distinct, idiosyncratic conflicts may contribute to asthma attacks.

AT is appended to Sessions 9–15 following the standard format as described in the clinical manual section of this book.

The results support the advantage of this procedure over a control group with standard medical (i.e., drug) treatment only. Treated patients were less anxious, perceived a lesser need to cough, and used fewer medications. Objective lung function parameters, however, did not show superiority over the drug-only group.

Stress Management

Another multicomponent package including AT has become the standard stress management approach in my own clinical work. The package has been successfully used with a variety of stress-related problems including hypertension, work-related burnout, migraine, low back pain, and generalized anxiety disorder. Although such treatment requires tailoring to suit different target problems and patients, the overall approach consists of a number of shared steps and strategies. First, the client is provided with a rationale that describes stress as a three-step process involving environmental stress triggers, behavioral and cognitive responses to the challenge, and the ensuing physiological stress response. For each of the three elements of the stress process different intervention techniques are taught: (1) situational analysis for the identification of stress triggers and the use of stimulus control procedures to prevent such stress triggers; (2) modification of the acute response to challenge via cognitive restructuring and assertive skill training; and (3) acquisition of a behavioral coping skill for reducing the physiological and subjective arousal via AT. Learning to relax through autogenic training has desirable acute effects and tends to generalize insofar as patients typically learn to perceive themselves as being in control of their stress responses.

This in turn impacts positively on the way they perceive potential stress triggers and how they respond to them. The reader wanting to learn more about stress management techniques (in a manual format) is referred to Davis, Robbins, Eshelman, and McKay's excellent book (1982) on stress reduction.

Autogenic Biofeedback

A fourth treatment package has become known by its own, unique name. Autogenic biofeedback has been used effectively with migraine patients (Fahrion, 1978; Pikoff, 1984; Sargent, Green, & Walters, 1973). In Autogenic biofeedback autogenic formulas are paired with the monitoring and visual and/or auditory display of physiological activity. This combination of procedures is considered useful because biofeedback makes apparent which changes occur and AT is considered to be a tool for triggering change. The advantage of pooling both techniques is most obvious in the early stages of training. The patient may be doing the right thing, but if he or she is not yet sensitized to his or her body sensations, the sensory feedback lacks salience.

A richly detailed description of the standard procedure has been provided by Fahrion (1978), an adapted version of which is presented below.*

Training Procedure for Autogenic Biofeedback

Prior to beginning biofeedback training each potential trainee should have a medical workup to establish the diagnosis of vascular or tension-vascular headache. These workups are carefully reviewed by the trainer before he sees the patient; and so

*From "Autogenic Biofeedback Treatment for Migraine" by S.L. Fahrion, 1978, *Research in Clinical Studies of Headache*, 5, pp. 63–68. Copyright 1978 by S. Karger AG. Adapted by permission.

a minimum amount of time is required for intake and diagnosis when the patient arrives for training.

The first 15–20 minutes of the initial appointment are spent developing rapport with the trainee and introducing the concept of biofeedback training. Particular emphasis is placed on explaining how biofeedback is applied to the trainee's specific disorder—that is, what body functions are being measured and how the normalization of these functions can help to alleviate the symptoms. Migraine sufferers referred for training have typically undergone a variety of different treatments without successful results and often feel somewhat hopeless or skeptical about the prospects for improving their condition. Therefore the trainee is shown several graphs of successful training programs with the intent of inducing a sense of hopefulness and positive expectancy about the treatment process.

The trainer also informs the client that positive results are likely, provided that two criteria are met: (1) the trainee must perform hand-warming exercises every day and must be able to sustain a hand temperature of at least 95.5°F for 10 minutes at a time; and (2) he should be able to increase hand temperature at a rate of at least 1°F per minute. (These criteria are perhaps somewhat more stringent than those currently required by most biofeedback practitioners, but the maintenance of these criteria is considered to be important if the best clinical results are to be obtained.)

During the first appointment the trainee is monitored for baseline levels of skin temperature and frontalis electromyogram (EMG). The EMG baseline data are especially important for individuals with mixed migraine and tension headaches. Since the initial training is usually performed with the patient lying down, the initial baseline data are also obtained in this position. Each physiological function is monitored over a 3-minute period, with successive readings taken every 20 seconds with a digital integrator and then averaged.

Many trainers place the skin temperature sensor on the first phalanx of the middle finger of the nondominant hand. The author prefers the sensor on the first phalanx of the little finger of the nondominant hand, since it has been observed that the little finger is the most sensitive to autonomic arousal mechanisms (it both warms and cools first), and the nondominant hand usually warms more rapidly than the dominant. This placement point is used for both baseline evaluation and for training.

As soon as baseline data are obtained, the trainee is oriented to the training process, with remarks such as the following: "At this point I'm going to give you some autogenic training phrases, and I want you to say each phrase over to yourself. Your attitude as you do this is quite important. This is the kind of thing where the more you try to relax, the less it will happen. So the best approach is to have the intention to become warm and relaxed, but to remain detached about your actual results. Since everyone can learn voluntary control of these processes, I would surmise that it is just a matter of time until you do, and therefore you can afford to be detached about the results.

"Saying these phrases is good because it keeps them in mind, but this is not enough. The part of the brain that controls these processes doesn't understand language, so it is important to translate the content of the phrase into some kind of an image. One of the phrases is, 'My hands are heavy and warm.' If you can actually imagine what it would feel like if your hands did feel heavy or if they did feel warm, that helps to bring on the changes. Or use a visual image. Imagine that you are lying out on the beach in the sun, or that you're holding hands over a campfire. Whatever works for you as a relaxing image is the thing to use, but the imagining itself is also important. Finally, if you simply trust your body to do what you're asking it to do, then you will discover that it will."

The modified autogenic training phrases developed by

the Menninger Foundation Voluntary Controls Project (Table 2) are then administered for approximately 20 minutes.

During the first training session only verbal feedback is given because direct instrument feedback commonly induces performance anxiety on the part of the trainee at this stage. Therefore, the trainer observes the physiological response on the instrument and provides verbal feedback that encourages improvement in hand temperature between each autogenic training phrase. The trainee might be told, "You are beginning to get warmer," and "You're now warming more rapidly," as these events occur. At each stage the trainee is given encouragement and reinforcement, but, at least initially, verbal feedback is not given when temperature decreases. Each time the trainee's hand temperature rises by 0.1°F he or she is informed that this has occurred. If the temperature is increasingly rapidly the trainee is told, "You've gone up 0.3°, 0.5°, 1°F, and so forth. It has been observed that some trainees experience very rapid increases in hand temperature, up to 3–4°F/minute.

During the first training session it is especially important that the autogenic training phrases be carefully placed to cor-

Table 2. Autogenic Phrases

I feel quiet...I am beginning to feel quite relaxed...My feet feel heavy and relaxed...My ankles, my knees, and my hips, feel heavy, relaxed, and comfortable...My solar plexus, and the whole central portion of my body, feel relaxed and quiet...My hands, my arms, and my shoulders, feel heavy, relaxed, and comfortable...My neck, my jaws, and my forehead feel relaxed...They feel comfortable and smooth...My whole body feels quiet, heavy, comfortable and relaxed.

I am quite relaxed...My arms and hands are heavy and warm...I feel quite quiet...My whole body is relaxed and my hands are warm, relaxed and warm...My hands are warm ...Warmth is flowing into my hands, they are warm...warm.

Note. From "Autogenic Biofeedback Treatment for Migraine" by S. L. Fahrion, 1978, *Research in Clinical Studies of Headache, 5*, p. 65. Copyright 1978 by S. Karger AG. Reprinted by permission.

respond to the trainee's actual physiological changes. If it appears that he or she is receiving special benefit from a particular phrase, no new phrase will be introduced for a period, and the trainee will be allowed to continue with that phrase until the rate of temperature increase begins to slow down, at which point the next phrase will be introduced. If it appears that a phrase is not producing the desired response, a new phrase may be introduced sooner than usual, or that phrase might be repeated. It is important for the trainee to be given sufficient time between phrases to be able to repeat each phrase slowly at least three times.

Toward the end of the first session auditory feedback will be introduced. Various instruments provide different forms of feedback, but the most widely used is a tone that decreases in pitch as the hands warm. Another sensitive and useful form of feedback is a tone that increases in pitch as the rate of warming increases. Should a trainee show a temperature decline the trainer might say, "There's been a slight temperature decrease, and there is nothing to do but to wait. Then it will turn around and you will begin to warm again." At the conclusion of the first training period the trainee is asked to open his or her eyes and the remainder of the session is devoted to discussing the experience, unhooking the instruments, and assigning homework exercises.

Subsequent training sessions generally follow the same course as the first session, with baseline data being taken at the beginning of each session. A typical appointment lasts an hour and consists of 20 minutes of training and 40 minutes of discussion. During the course of the therapy a variety of factors may arise that the trainee might wish to discuss, such as the nature of the symptoms, changes that are occurring as a result of therapy, and so forth. It is important for the trainee to feel that the therapist is genuinely interested and willing to listen to any problems or issues he or she wishes to bring up. This discussion must be kept within reason, however, and not be allowed to generate excessive distraction from the training.

In the case of individuals with tension headaches or mixed tension/migraine headaches, an alternative procedure is used. During the first two sessions EMG activity is monitored while the trainee performs temperature training with the autogenic phrases. If there is a high correlation between temperature increase and EMG decrease during these sessions, temperature training is continued as a sole feedback modality. If not, training is divided between temperature and EMG, with temperature training performed first. During the initial stages of EMG training verbal feedback is used, while audio feedback is gradually introduced at a low volume. No phrases or other special procedures are used during EMG training. The trainee is simply permitted to use the audio feedback to keep informed of his or her progress toward relaxed levels.

After each session the therapist makes a graph of the trainee's progress during that session using the information taken down from the instruments during the training period. At the point when it is clear that the trainee is beginning to

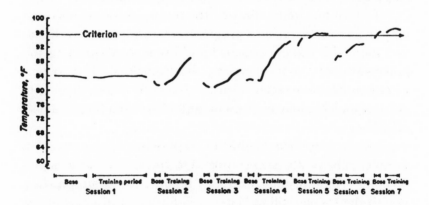

Figure 5. Hand temperature in a 43-year-old man undergoing autogenic biofeedback training. From "Autogenic Biofeedback Treatment for Migraine" by S. L. Fahrion, 1978, *Research in Clinical Studies of Headache, 5,* p. 67. Copyright 1978 by S. Karger AG. Reprinted by permission.

show progress, these graphs are shown to the trainee, since they serve to reinforce a sense of accomplishment. Figure 5 illustrates the complete course of temperature training with a 43-year-old man referred for general relaxation training in relation to a variety of stress-related problems.

Some attention must be paid to the integration of the results of this practice into the daily life of the trainee. Homework practice is considered imperative in facilitating a generalization of training skills. At the end of the first session each individual being treated for headache is given a daily "diary" in which to chart headache activity hourly. The material from these sheets is subsequently averaged on a weekly basis and presented on a graph for the trainee's review. He or she is also given cassette tapes of the autogenic phrases, which should be taken home and practiced as often as possible, but at least once a day. As soon as the trainee begins to demonstrate a capacity for temperature self-regulation, he or she is given an inexpensive monitoring device for home use. Hand temperature is recorded at the beginning and at the end of each homework practice session, and these results are reviewed by the trainer each week.

To facilitate generalization the trainee moves to a sitting-up position as the sessions progress—first with the eyes closed, and then with the eyes open. In addition to performing the homework relaxation exercises, the trainee is asked to perform a mental body scan at various intervals of the day to note any tension that may be present, and to spend a few moments relaxing.

When a trainee begins to experience the onset of a headache, he or she is encouraged to spend 1–2 minutes performing hand-warming exercises before taking any medication. If the trainee still feels the need for medication, he or she takes it. As soon as the medication begins to take effect, the hand-warming exercises are performed again. (The purpose of this procedure is to maximize the effect of the medication and to establish a conditioned association between hand warming and headache relief.) The trainee is asked to discontinue the medication at the onset of biofeedback training, and, in fact, is asked to attempt to reduce all medication as other suffers have been able to markedly reduce their dosages.

Those who habitually awaken with a migraine headache are asked to set their alarm clocks to a time midway through their regular sleeping period, and to note whether or not there are any headache symptoms when they awake. If so, they perform hand-warming exercises before returning to sleep. If not, they set their alarm clock for a later time in an attempt to pinpoint the time when the symptoms occur. (It is known that hand temperature varies considerably during dream periods, and it is considered possible that dream content may be a source of many of the headache symptoms that originate during sleep.)

The final session includes a discussion of the training progress achieved thus far, as well as an orientation about what remains to be done. The patient is instructed to maintain a hand temperature of 95.5°F for at least 10 minutes each day. The maintenance of deep, autonomic relaxation associated with high hand temperature is the factor that most effectively protects the individual from migraine attacks by helping to establish a more normal psychophysiological posture. The trainee continues to send the therapist headache report cards for the next few months. If it appears from these headache reports that he or she is experiencing difficulties, or if the cards are not sent, the therapist telephones to inquire about his or her progress and to recommend whatever modifications in training methodology seem appropriate. As a routine procedure, the therapist telephones each trainee after several months for a follow-up evaluation.

An early outcome evaluation suggests that autogenic biofeedback is quite effective for migraine but not for tension

headache (Green et al., 1975). In a later outcome study subjects were randomly assigned to either (1) a no-treatment wait-
list control, (2) AT, (3) EMG biofeedback and AT, or (4) temperature biofeedback with AT (Sargent, Solback, Coyne,
Spohn, & Segersen, 1986). The results confirmed the earlier
findings of the effectiveness of autogenic biofeedback. Direct
outcome comparisons of autogenic biofeedback versus standard AT (i.e., without the biofeedback component) and versus
other techniques are discussed in more detail in Chapter 13,
which deals with controlled therapy outcome research.

Part III
Supporting Research

⟡ 12 ⟡

Research Supporting Autogenic Principles

This chapter is concerned with the question of whether or not Schultz's claim for formula-specific training effects has been experimentally demonstrated. A variety of research strategies are necessary to comprehensively investigate whether or not the use of autogenic formulas brings about the expected change in physiological activity. The initial question is whether patients (or any trainees for that matter) actually experience on a subjective level the suggestions made in the autogenic formulas. If so, it is also necessary to demonstrate that specific physiological changes accompany the suggested, subjective experiences. The argument for specificity can be considered supported when distinct physiological changes exclusively accompany those formulas that suggest them, but are not observed during the practice of other formulas.

Also of clinical importance is the additional question of whether the acute imagery of an autogenic state is sufficient to provoke clinically meaningful changes, or whether long-term training is required for clinical benefit. Lastly there is the debate about whether or not physiological changes during AT are unique to AT or are observed equally in other relaxation/biobehavioral treatments like biofeedback, meditation, muscular relaxation, or Benson's relaxation response. Extreme positions on this issue are taken by Benson (1975) on one side, who argues for an equivalence of effects across diverse methods, and by Woolfolk and Lehrer (1984) on the other, who see specificity associated with different biobehavioral methods. Clarification of this specificity question is of considerable importance to clinicians because method specificity would require a careful matching of the problem and patient personality to potential treatment options, whereas Benson's (1975) claim for the universality of relaxation effects implies little need for fine-tuned tailoring in treatment decisions. All of these questions are relevant to the attempt to prove the credibility of AT as an effective and unique method of change. This chapter is devoted to seeking answers for these questions in the experimental literature and to discussing the implications of findings for clinical and research applications.

Subjective Experiences of Autogenic States

Mensen (1975) has provided pertinent data on the subjective experiences of autogenic states. The quality of perceived autogenic sensations was rated by 150 participants of a six-session (2 hours each) training program. After the six sessions 100% of the participants reported the suggested sensations of "heaviness," "warmth," "heart regularity," and "breathing regularity." "Sunrays warm" was reported by 90% and "cool forehead" was reported by 70% of the participants. Although one may be tempted to call this kind of self-report nothing but self-fulfilling prophecy, the figures are further supported by spontaneous reports of untrained generalization effects. That is, patients who had not yet been trained in some of the later formulas nevertheless reported these sensations. For example, 40% of the participants spontaneously experienced the breathing sensation, and 50% reported the sunray sensation before either was taught. Heaviness and warmth experiences were evident in all participants after only three training sessions. Because these autogenic experiences have been reported by patients before they were actually instructed in them, it appears that the autogenic formulas, at least in part, form a cluster of typically co-occurring bodily sensations that are experienced when trainees practice. The specificity argument therefore receives little support from the literature on subjective experience. These findings do, however, support the claim that the autogenic sensations per se can be reliably acquired and promptly produced by nearly all trainees. The "forehead cool" formula is clearly the most difficult to learn.

Behavioral Indices of AT States

Surprisingly, the AT literature is void of discussions on how the depth and experience of AT formulas can be determined behaviorally. One would expect researchers to be interested in correlating subjective sensations, measurable physiological events, and overt behavioral indices while studying AT mechanisms. Ideally, all levels of observation will match up and suggest a coherent pattern of systematic changes during AT practice. However, the emphasis in measuring the effects and progress of AT has been on determining subjective feelings of change and their physiological correlates. In the absence of systematic studies on overt behavioral change during AT, related studies in the relaxation literature may serve as a window into the behavioral phenomena. One scale that seems particularly suitable to assess behavioral changes during AT is reprinted here (Table 3). Luiselli, Steinman, Marholin, and Steinman (1981) have used the scale to evaluate relaxation ef-

Table 3. Scale of Behavioral Markers of Relaxation

1. Forehead		
Deeply furrowed or wrinkled	5 4 3 2 1	Smooth
2. Eyes		
Deeply wrinkled, squeezed tightly	5 4 3 2 1	Loosely closed, almost fluttering
3. Neck		
Veins or muscles visible, extended	5 4 3 2 1	Smooth
4. Head		
Held straight, centered	5 4 3 2 1	Tilted to one side or forward
5. Arms		
Close to body or shoulders raised	5 4 3 2 1	On chair arms or lap or away from body, shoulders forward
6. Hands		
Closed fist, clenching chair, tapping	5 4 3 2 1	Open, palms up, resting on lap or chair arms
7. Legs		
Close together, swaying, wiggling	5 4 3 2 1	Apart, kness out, no movement
8. Feet		
Together, flat on floor, tapping	5 4 3 2 1	Apart, resting on heels, toes pointing out
9. Breathing		
Rapid, uneven	5 4 3 2 1	Slow, even

Note. From "Evaluation of Progressive Muscle Relaxation with Conduct-Problem, Learning-Disabled Children" by J. K. Luiselli, D. L. Steinman, D. Marholin II, and W. M. Steinman, 1981, *Child Behavior Therapy, 3*, p. 45. Copyright 1981 by The Haworth Press. Reprinted by permission.

fects in children, and it taps a variety of important, easy-to-detect features of the relaxation process.

Physiological Specificity for Each AT Formula

Numerous researchers have investigated whether the suggested formula-specific sensations reflect parallel physiological changes. For an overview, supporting studies and their key findings are summarized in Table 4.

The studies summarized here confirm that the desired effects do occur during the particular exercises intended to trigger them, but it is clearly bad science to look only for confirmatory evidence. Good science (Kuhn, 1970), by contrast, will also investigate the mechanism behind a given phenomenon, will seek other potential explanations, and will demonstrate the strength of the presumed cause–effect relationship (i.e., the practice of an AT formula and the subsequent physiological change) by ruling out alternative explana-

Table 4. Physiological Changes during Autogenic Training

Training Step	Physiological effects	References
1. Heaviness (muscular relaxation)	Reduction of muscle tone, and blood pressure, increase in skin resistance	Fischel & Mueller, 1962; Ohno, 1965; Schultz, 1973; von Siebenthal, 1952: Wallnoefer, 1972
2. Warmth (vascular dilation)	Peripheral vasodilation in hands and face; increase in skin temperature; occasional light sweating	Dobeta et al., 1966; Peliccioni & Liebner, 1980; Polzien, 1974; Schwarz & Langen, 1966
3. Heart (regulation of heart activity)	Reduction of heart rate; cardiac output with simultaneously improved O_2-utilization; stabilization of labile electrocardiograms	Luthe, 1970; Polzien, 1953
4. Breathing (regulation of breathing)	Reduction of breathing volume and frequency; shift from thoracic to abdominal breathing	Ikemi et al., 1965; Linden, 1977; Luthe, 1970; Polzein,
5. Sunrays (regulation of visceral organ activity)	Normalization of disturbed and/or irritable stomach and intestines; increased blood flow to gastric mucous; additional vasodilation of peripheral vessels	Ikemi et al, 1965; Sapir & Reverchon, 1965; Lantzsch & Drunkenmoelle, 1975
6. Cool forehead (regulation of the head)	Reduction of beta- and increase of alpha- and theta-waves in the electroencephalogram	Geismann, 1968; Israel & Rohmer, 1958; Jus & Jus, 1968; Katzenstein, 1967

tions. Although the studies listed in Table 4 provide empirical support for the idea that the suggested autogenic effects are typically achieved, one cannot conclude that they can only be achieved either by use of the specific formula or through AT. A more fine-grained analysis of the literature is required to deal with all of the relevant aspects of the specificity question. In order to achieve this, a brief review of the physiological changes to be expected from biobehavioral treatments similar to AT (i.e., muscular relaxation, Benson's relaxation response, meditation) is provided below. The demonstrated physiological changes during AT are discussed next, and findings from direct method comparisons are then considered to identify the specificity of AT effects.

Physiological Effects of Alternative Self-regulation Methods in Healthy Individuals

Empirical data on the acute effects of various forms of relaxation training have been available for quite some time (Benson, 1975; Borkovec & Fowles, 1973; Wallace & Benson, 1972). They have also been replicated and compared with one another (Lehrer, Woolfolk, Rooney, et al., 1983; Paul, 1969; Woolfolk, Lehrer, McCann, & Rooney, 1982), and an excellent review is provided elsewhere (Lehrer & Woolfolk, 1984).

A seminal study on meditation effects was executed by Wallace (1970) comparing physiological changes in 15 experienced healthy meditators in a within-subject design: The meditators were studied during simple resting phases, during the practice of meditation, and again during a subsequent resting phase. The observed physiological changes were statistically significant and of considerable magnitude, and the findings were further strengthened by the fact that during simple resting (which has basic metabolic demands similar to those of meditation) little change was noted. Some of the key findings are displayed in Table 5.

Table 5. Physiological Changes during Transcendental Meditation.

Time sequence	O$_2$ consumption (cm³/min)	Respiratory quotient	Minute ventilation (liter/min)	Skin resistance (kilohm)
		Resting		
10	246.8	0.86	5.90	91.2
20	244.4	0.87	7.56	101.2
		Meditation		
35	208.1	0.84	5.25	205.0
45	201.9	0.85	5.28	188.8
55	200.8	0.85	5.55	180.1
		Resting		
70	233.1	0.86	5.94	80.2

Note. The values given represent the mean for all subjects tested. The resting values are typical for normal subjects. From "Physiological Effects of Transcendental Meditation" by R. K. Wallace, 1970, *Science,* 167, pp. 1753. Copyright 1970 by the American Association for the Advancement of Science. Reprinted by permission.

In addition to the meditation-induced changes in skin resistance and respiratory activity, decreases in heart rate and changes in electroencephalographic (EEG) activity patterns were observed. EEG activity clearly differed from both sleeping and wakeful activity patterns in that alpha-wave dominance, without delta waves or sleep spindles, was observed.

Because all of Wallace's (1970) subjects were experienced meditators with 6 months to 3 years of experience, it was not clear whether brief relaxation would provoke similarly distinct physiological changes. One representative study dealing with this question was executed by Paul (1969), who compared three groups: (1) a self-relaxation group that served as a control and simply rested; (2) a group using hypnotic induction which suggested feelings of heaviness, drowsiness, warmth, relaxation; and (3) a group using abbreviated muscular relaxation. Participants received only two training sessions, and changes were monitored throughout both sessions. Both forms of active relaxation were clearly more effective in reducing autonomic arousal than was the control condition. This finding suggests that even brief relaxation training can be sufficient to trigger arousal reductions that exceed simple resting activity, thereby strengthening the argument that relaxation training possesses a specificity of effects exceeding simple resting. The argument for specificity was further strengthened by Paul's (1969) finding that hypnotic suggestions were slower and less effective in reducing respiratory rate, heart rate, and muscle tension than was muscular relaxation. Comparisons of relaxation methods that share self-induction as a feature (i.e. trancendental meditation, biofeedback, muscular relaxation, the relaxation reponse), showed that in healthy populations relaxation was easily learned by most trainees, and that different methods shared general stress-reducing effects but also showed method-specific effects (Lehrer & Woolfolk, 1984). (Note that controlled, clinical comparions involving AT are discussed only in the chapter on therapy outcome.) Lehrer and Woolfolk concluded that muscular relaxation produced effects specific to the musculoskeletal system, that biofeedback was most effective on the particular autonomic function addressed in a given training program, that biofeedback and muscular relaxation had stronger somatic effects than did meditation, and that *training* subjects to relax produced greater somatic effects than simply *suggesting* that subjects (via hypnosis, for example) relax. As a whole, these findings justify the inference that AT will have similar stress-reducing effects, and that it may have unique, method-specific advantages. These, however, will be difficult to detect because they are part and parcel of an already effective technique that shares at least some of its effects with other methods. In the next section AT effects will be reviewed, and in the final section of this chapter contrasted with changes produced through similar biobehavioral treatments.

Physiological Effects of AT on Healthy Individuals

A number of studies have been executed to test the acute effects of AT in typically healthy individuals. Findings from these studies are summarized below and are organized alphabetically according to the physiological target indices. Observations from single-case studies and/or seemingly uncontrolled group studies are left out of this review because they are perceived to contribute little when controlled research is available.

Blood volume changes during the heaviness and warmth formulas have been studied by Pelliccioni and Liebner (1980) via ultrasound and Doppler-sonography. Six trainees were fully trained in the six standard formulas and the three control subjects were unfamiliar with AT. Pelliccioni and Liebner (1980) reported no blood volume changes in the untrained subjects, whereas noticeable increases in systolic volume amplitude and overall blood flow were reported using the warmth exercise in the trained subjects. Furthermore, the blood flow changes were equally noted in the targeted area (the arm) and in the cerebral vasculature, thus suggesting a generalization of the effect beyond the target area.

Cholesterol changes during AT were reported by Aya (1967) who compared junior high school students who were classified as either successful (*N*=12) or unsuccessful (*N*=10) in producing autogenic sensations. Change was studied over a 4-week period during which subjects practiced the warmth and heaviness exercises. The successful AT group showed a 19% reduction in cholesterol values, which represented a significant change from the baseline. The unsuccessful group showed only a 3% reduction, such that posttest values did not significantly differ from the baselines. The observed reductions in cholesterol show promise for the use of AT as a preventive method for heart disease, and the observation of cholesterol reduction in the successful group suggests that the subjective training experience may represent a valid index of accompanying physiological change.

Acute *cortisol* changes in three experimental groups were noted by Alnaes (1966). Ten subjects were controls who rested without any additional instruction, twelve subjects received heterohypnotic relaxation instructions, and thirteen subjects (who had previously learned all six standard AT formulas) used the heaviness and warmth formulas. After a 4-minute relaxation phase using one of these three relaxation methods, all subjects were exposed to a 15-minute stress task consisting of unpredictable bell sounds and pin pricks. AT-trained subjects displayed a smaller cortisol response to the task than did the other groups, who also showed relatively larger variability in their cortisol responses. This result is of interest because cortisol is not directly addressed by any of the autogenic formulas, but is considered to be a major index in physiological stress responding (Dienstbier, 1989), thus underlining the potential of AT to reduce stress physiologically.

Increased *skin resistance* has been reliably observed during acute AT practice. Fischel and Mueller (1962) studied electrodermal activity (EDA) in 20 fully AT-trained psychotherapy patients and noted rapid and smooth increases in skin resistance that leveled off after 3–4 minutes of AT practice. Although EDA is known to be highly sensitive to sensory challenges, these researchers noted little effect from outside noise disturbances on the stability of the EDA, thus confirming the stable state of "detachedness" of the trainees. Ohno (1965) replicated these findings using 36 patients with either neurotic or psychosomatic symptomatology. Mean increases in skin resistance were observed in 31 of the 36 patients whereas only two showed no change, and three displayed decreased resistance. Braud and Masters (1980) tested for the specificity of effects by studying how EDA responds to opposite types of imagery. Fifteen healthy, untrained subjects received tape-recorded instructions for relaxation imagery suggesting quietude, heaviness, warmth, coolness of the forehead, calmness, and regularity of breathing and circulation, while fifteen control subjects were exposed to the opposite suggestions. Directionally appropriate changes were reported for three aspects of EDA, thus suggesting that the inappropriate imagery indeed had differential effects. As a whole, these studies indicate EDA changes consistent with the desired relaxation effect of AT and even untrained subjects displayed the desired change after brief instructions (Braud & Masters, 1980).

Electroencephalographic (EEG) changes during AT have been studied by a variety of research groups. Unfortunately, the methods of obtaining and interpreting EEGs vary from lab to lab and the respective literature is not conducive to making easy comparisons. Nevertheless, some key findings appear with consistency. There is replicated evidence from studying EEG changes in trained subjects that AT reliably triggers such changers. These indicate relaxation and are—at least initially—similar to changes observed with meditation (Wallace, 1970). Increased frequency of theta and delta waves, predominance of alpha waves, and synchronicity in wave forms of varying frequencies were observed (Israel & Rohmer, 1958; Jus & Jus, 1968; Katzenstein, 1967; Sipos, Bodo, Nagypal, & Tomka, 1978), thus marking a clear difference between relaxation and mentally active states. Jus and Jus (1968) reported an increasing differentiation between AT-induced EEG activity and that provoked by hypnosis, and found that the alpha dominance became more pronounced with AT.

Recently, Jacobs and Lubar (1989) examined the acute effects of AT using power spectrum analysis of the EEG. Twenty-eight healthy subjects were divided into two experimental groups, one receiving fifteen sessions of AT with home practice, while the second (the control) group received the same number of treatment sessions, but only listened to a pleasant radio show and did not engage in home practice. EEG measures were taken to monitor long-term change (that is, compared resting state EEGs before and after treatment), and acute changes based on EEG activity during the practice of AT in the lab were also monitored. The results suggested clear acute effect differences between the groups. AT-trained subjects showed greater increases in theta and greater increases in alpha percent power. The findings also indicated that AT practice produced systematic EEG changes over time and also triggered a pattern of acute brain-wave activity that was distinguishable from the pattern seen in control subjects who also relaxed but were untrained in AT. Thus overall as well as specific effects could be demonstrated. Jacobs and Lubar's (1989) findings thus replicate and confirm earlier observations of EEG activity during AT practice.

A further method of studying brain activity during AT is through auditory or visually evoked potential (Dongier, Debosseley, Rousseau, & Timsit-Berthier, 1967), which have provided evidence of the differences between AT and hypnosis. Reticular activation (a sign of increased vigilance) was uniquely observed during AT, and furthermore, AT-trained subjects displayed more accentuated habituation to auditory stimulation of evoked potentials (Dongier et al., 1967).

Electrocardiographic (ECG) evaluations of 35 heart patients with clinically important depressions of the ST segment of their ECGs were undertaken by Polzien (1953) while these patients were practicing the heaviness formula of AT. ECGs were derived before, during, and after the practice session. Practice of the heaviness formula was associated with an average decrease of 4 beats per minute in heart rate, and in 28 of the 35 patients the ST segment was elevated by at least 0.05 mV. It appears that even the use of a single AT formula has acute, beneficial effects on the cardiac function of patients with diagnosed cardiovascular risk.

Electromyographic (EMG) changes were studied by von Siebenthal (1952) in 20 subjects who practiced the heaviness formula but were instructed to specifically target the left, the right, or both arms simultaneously. Findings revealed that muscle potential decreased (i.e., relaxation was apparent) in nearly all subjects and that training both arms simultaneously was more effective than single arm training. These findings support the suggested effect of the heaviness formula on muscle tone.

Fine body movement determined via a static sensograph was studied in 30 healthy Japanese adolescents who were either untrained controls or trained in AT for 4.5 months (Tebecis et al., 1976/77; 1977). Fine body movement is not a frequently studied physiological index. It refers to body movements that are correlates of attempts to maintain balance and that therefore may be due to subtle muscular activity. Fine body movement is apparently greater when individuals are fatigued and anxious, thus suggesting it may be a useful gross index of "stress." In the AT group, but not the controls, fine body movement decreased steadily with increased training frequency and was significantly different from baseline after 3 and after 4.5 months of training. The AT group also displayed distinct EEG changes and increasing blood flow in the hands. Tebecis et al. (1977) also noted that the blood flow improvements were only apparent in those trainees who reported subjective increases in temperature. The authors concluded that fine body movement may be a useful and sensitive outcome index for relaxation training at large.

Gastrointestinal complaints and their acute modifiability via AT were studied in ten individual patients who had learned the complete AT procedure. X-ray examinations were undertaken before and during the practice of AT and revealed clinically meaningful improvements in gastrointestinal motility throughout the esophagus, stomach, duodenum, and jejunum regions (Sapir & Reverchon, 1965). Not enough detail was provided with the report to isolate the timing and effect of specific formulas on the gastrointestinal motility improvements.

Heart rate changes during AT have been the focus of numerous researchers' attention (Blizard, Cowings & Miller, 1975; Luthe, 1970a; Polzien, 1953; Shapiro & Lehrer, 1980). Shapiro and Lehrer's study was a method comparison between abbreviated AT and muscular relaxation and will therefore be discussed in a later section of this chapter on method comparisons. Unfortunately, the authors did not report the raw data or means of heart rate changes during the acute practice of AT.

Polzien's (1953) findings on heart rate change have already been mentioned in the section on electrocardiographic changes during AT. Use of the heaviness formula only triggered an average decrease of 4 beats per minute in the heart rate in a group of diagnosed heart patients. Another study investigated fifteen neurotic patients after 4 weeks of heaviness training. After the establishment of a baseline by having them rest with their eyes closed for 180 seconds and taking a measurement, the subjects used the heaviness formula (Luthe, 1970a). Average heart rate during the exercise was 5% lower than the resting baseline readings. Blizard et al. (1975) tested autonomic specificity by suggesting opposite types of imagery to nine healthy subjects who were trained in six daily sessions. The contrasting suggestions were "warm and heavy" or "light and cool." The "cool" instruction reliably increased the heart rate (+4 beats/min.) and respiration rate (+1 cycle/min.) above baseline values whereas the "warm" instructions led to nonsignificant decreases (−1 beats/min. and −1 cycle/min. respectively). Although Blizard et al.'s (1975) findings support the specificity argument, they provide little support for AT (heaviness and warmth) induced reductions in heart rate in healthy subjects. Both studies with clinical populations, however, showed reliable decreases in heart rates, thus suggesting that healthy subjects are already close to the floor of obtainable resting levels and do not leave much room for reduction in autonomic activity levels.

Respiration changes have been studied by Linden (1977) and Luthe (1970a). Luthe (1970a) trained 15 healthy subjects in the full AT package and studied respiratory changes within the training sessions while simultaneously recording the specific formulas that were used at given times. The findings are best demonstrated by reprinting the figures Luthe provided.

As can be seen in Figures 6 and 7, a variety of respiration indices change systematically with AT. They tend to be most pronounced, however, during the respiration exercise itself and then weaken during the progressing training steps such as

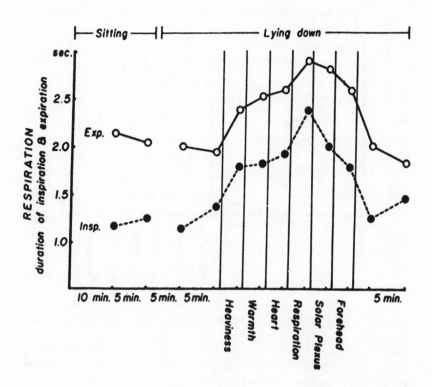

Figure 6. The influence of the standard exercises upon the duration of inspiration and expiration in 15 healthy trainees. From *Autogenic Therapy. Vol. IV: Research and Theory* by W. Luthe, 1970, New York: Grune & Stratton. Copyright 1970 by Grune & Stratton. Adapted by permission.

the solar plexus and forehead exercises. Both inspiration and expiration slow down during AT. The respiratory frequency decreases by about 5–6 cycles/min, abdominal amplitude increases, whereas thoracic amplitude remains unchanged.

These figures provide a lucid demonstration of how respiratory changes intensify with the deepening of the AT practice and peak during the respiration exercise. Luthe's results (1970a) represent a convincing argument for the combination

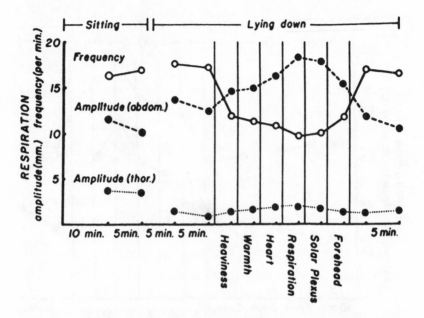

Figure 7. The influence of the standard exercises upon the respiratory frequency and the abdominal and thoracic amplitude in 15 healthy trainees. From *Autogenic Therapy. Vol. IV: Research and Theory* by W. Luthe, 1970, New York: Grune & Stratton. Copyright 1970 by Grune and Stratton. Adapted by permission.

of generalized and specific effects that occur during AT. The findings were replicated by Linden (1977) who trained 12 healthy individuals over a 3-month period in the full AT procedures. Respiratory frequency and CO_2 consumption were monitored and showed large decreases beginning with the heaviness formula. These were maintained throughout the acute training phase.

Skin temperature effects of acute AT practice have been thoroughly investigated by a variety of independent research groups (Dobeta, Sugaro, & Ohno, 1966; Hohn, 1966; Polzien, 1955; Schwarz & Langen, 1966). Skin temperature has been extensively studied for two reasons. The temperature at the skin surface is a good indicator of changes in underlying blood flow (that is, it reflects vasoconstrictive and vasodilatory processes), and it permits relatively easy, location-specific measurement. Freedman and Ianni (1983) also measured temperature changes during AT, but this was part of a clinical method comparison and will, therefore, be discussed in the following chapter.

Temperature changes in the finger, hand, and rectum of 37 psychosomatic patients practicing heaviness were studied by Polzien (1955). During the first minute of the heaviness practice temperature remained stable and then increased, reaching their respective peaks after 9–15 minutes, in average increments of +1.81°C. Finger temperature increased more than hand temperature whereas rectal temperature dropped slightly.

Schwarz and Langen (1966) reported a series of studies. The first was on 12 healthy students who had learned and practiced the complete AT procedure. The subjects' arms were exposed to low room temperatures (manipulated to be between 0° and +10°C) for 2 hours. Subsequent practice of the heaviness and warmth formulas showed temperature increases and simultaneous augmentation of blood volume by a ratio of 1:3. The training effect on temperature increases was weakened when the room was cooler: at 7°–10°C 77% of subjects effectively raised their hand temperature, but this figure dropped to 62% at 3°–6°C, and to 54% at 0°–2°C room temperature. The findings underline the gradient effect of autogenic temperature changes, which are more difficult, but still possible, to achieve in cold environments.

In a second study the same authors compared objective and subjective temperature changes in three groups of subjects who had either (1) learned AT and reported strong warmth sensations ($N = 62$), (2) had been exposed to active hypnosis and reported warmth ($N = 22$), or (3) had learned AT but reported difficulties with warmth sensations ($N = 44$). The primary result of the comparison was that subjective warmth sensations strongly and positively correlated with objective temperature increases.

Hohn (1966) focused on the single and combined effects of AT's heaviness and warmth formulas and of a vasodilating drug in 15 healthy volunteers. Though both manipulations raised hand temperatures, the combined effects were greater than those of a single intervention, and the most effective order of presenting interventions was drug first and AT second. When AT-trained neurotic and psychosomatic patients ($N = 35$) were studied by Dobeta et al. (1966) during practice of the warmth formula, 91.4% of these patients showed an acute rise in finger temperature.

In summary, these studies document reliable temperature increases with the AT warmth formula. The effect was weakened but still present when the room temperature approached freezing, and the subjective warmth experience consistently correlated with measurable temperature increases in the same site. The findings do not, however, reveal to what degree temperature changes are also apparent during the practice of other AT formulas.

Comparison of Acute Physiological Changes during AT versus Other Biobehavioral Interventions

Shapiro and Lehrer (1980) taught progressive muscular relaxation or AT (heaviness, warmth, and respiration formulas only) for 5 weeks to groups of 11 healthy subjects each, while a group of $N = 10$ subjects served as no-treatment controls. Both types of training reduced subjective anxiety, depression, and the frequency and intensity of physical symptoms. AT produced specific effects on self-perceived heaviness and warmth, as well as on the depth of breathing. Active treatments were not different from one another with respect to heart rate or skin conductance changes from pre- to post-test.

Two comparison studies were executed on hand warming: Kelton and Belar (1983) trained healthy children, whereas

Freedman and Ianni (1983) trained healthy adults. Twenty-six child subjects were divided into two training groups ($N = 13$ each) and all received four 35–45 minute training sessions on 4 consecutive days (Kelton & Belar, 1983). Both groups received tape-recorded instructions for hand-warming (heaviness and warmth formulas), but only one group received simultaneous biological feedback as well. Training effects were not different for the two treatments, no significant hand warming occurred from stabilization to training phase (i.e., within the session), but both groups displayed increased temperatures during the stabilization phase when days 1, 3, and 4 were compared.

Freedman and Ianni (1983) reported two studies with 32 and 16 healthy subjects respectively. In the first study subjects receiving finger temperature feedback showed increases in digital temperature during the beginning of the first training session, whereas other subjects trained via audiotaped heaviness and warmth suggestions (AT), or EMG feedback, or instructions to raise finger temperature did not. During later sessions no training effect for any group was observed. At post-training (i.e., after six training sessions) only the temperature feedback group displayed voluntary control in the laboratory; no group displayed generalization outside of the lab. In the second study the basic design was duplicated but training periods and session length were reduced. The superiority of finger temperature feedback was now evident both inside as well as outside the lab.

The results of comparisons of AT with other methods are disappointing at first glance because few if any specific effects are reported, and because AT effects appear to be neither distinct nor superior. Inspection of the design characteristics, however, raises grave doubts about the power of these studies to detect potential differences. All used healthy volunteers (which enhanced the possibility of floor effects that would jeopardize finding overall change), and all used very brief, tape-recorded, and incomplete AT formulas.

Conclusions from the Basic Research Literature

A large body of literature attests to the multiple changes that occur during the acute practice of AT (that is, while trainees are using the AT formulas). Effects have been demonstrated on a wide range of physiological target indices. Failures to find effects were observed only in studies of healthy volunteers who typically had received minimal training that was further weakened by tape-recorded deliveries. Nevertheless, many effects, such as respiration and temperature changes, are apparent even in healthy individuals, provided that they master the complete AT procedures. Multiple evidence has been presented that the subjective experience of autogenic sensations is a reliable correlate of physiological changes. In summary, there is a great deal of evidence that well-taught AT produces the desired acute effects in dysfunctional and, to a lesser degree, in healthy populations, and thereby provides strong empirical support for AT's potential as a treatment for psychophysiologically based dysfunctions. The research to date suggests that training effects quickly and effectively generalize, thus making the empirical demonstration of formula-specific changes very difficult. Research comparing the acute effects of AT with other methods has shown no differences in healthy subjects, but this is likely due to restricted range problems typical for healthy populations, as well as flawed (i.e., audiotaped, modified, and extremely brief) AT training procedures.

This chapter was purposely devoted to experimental studies on the acute effects of AT in healthy and dysfunctional populations because the demonstration of the fact that AT can acutely trigger the intended effects is essential for the building of a treatment rationale. Once acute effects have been shown, AT (or any related technique for that matter) can then be applied in attempts to produce long-term, generalized treatment effects. Method comparisons of this type are reviewed in the next chapter.

⋄13⋄

Review of the Clinical Outcome Literature

This chapter presents and discusses therapy outcome research on AT. This is done with an intended positive bias toward studies that are sufficiently well described to be replicable, that can be considered controlled (i.e., by the inclusion of some control group or by other widely accepted measures) and that are based on reasonably large patient samples (to permit generalizability). The underlying reason for this methodological bias is twofold.

   1. The available literature on AT is vast and suggests that AT has been effectively used for literally any medical/psychosomatic/psychiatric disorder that may possess a psychological component. These descriptions of a universally applicable treatment, and of its consistently positive outcomes, however, are frequently based on uncontrolled case studies and anec-

dotes, and while they may appear to be a panacea to the true believer, they may simultaneously raise suspicion in the hard-data-oriented clinical researcher. Before therapy studies are funded and before therapy programs become integrated into the health-service delivery routines, the effectiveness of the therapy needs to be demonstrated, and cost-benefit ratios, which are often called for by policymakers who control the budgets, need to be compiled. Case studies and clinical anecdotes count little in these respects, and an up-to-date review on controlled AT outcomes, which is sorely missing from the literature, might be difficult to amass, especially when one considers the need to review English and German material to achieve this end. There can be little doubt that the previously noted paucity of available, controlled, group outcome studies on AT (Pikoff, 1984) has hindered the maximal propagation of AT, especially in North America.

2. This review of outcome will also highlight whether or not procedures have followed a standard script (as suggested by Luthe, for example) and have provided training of the desired length. Pikoff (1984) has suggested that many studies listed under AT in the medical and psychological index systems use abbreviated and/or modified versions of AT. An inspection of Pikoff's summary tables revealed that of the 30 listed therapy studies, 12 had used only formulas 1 and 2 (heaviness and warmth) and 7 did not specify which formulas had been used. This raises the question of whether standardized AT for a given disorder has ever been empirically tested with a sound, controlled design without such modifications and abbreviations being used. At the risk of being called a purist, I refuse to consider a method tested unless the original, standardized procedure has been used in well-controlled clinical studies. Therefore, a review that concentrates on controlled group trials and presents the findings in a lucid and concise manner is needed. After the completion of such review on the standardized use of AT, the areas of application where AT has been properly tested with replicated findings will also become clear. Alternatively,

some treatment applications are highlighted in this chapter even though the available findings are based on flawed (non-standardized, too short, or incomplete) procedures. Taken together, this approach to the research literature is expected to direct future researchers into the areas of greatest need and facilitate the necessary accumulation of a sound knowledge base (Linden & Wen, in press), and in turn help to establish the clinical value of AT.

In order to achieve the above objectives, only studies with the following minimal characteristics were considered for the critical evaluation of AT in this chapter:

1. Inclusion of a control group or phase (either no-treatment control, placebo, alternative treatment, or within-subject control [like A-B-A-B design]).
2. At least $N = 5$ in the smallest group tested.
3. Inclusion of at least one standardized, widely accepted outcome measure for a given dysfunction.

Strict application of such minimal exclusion criteria reveals the many substantial flaws in this literature. When for example, the 30 English-language studies described by Pikoff (1984) are subjected to these elementary criteria for good outcome research, nine need to be excluded because they lack control groups, an additional six are single case studies, and seven do not specify the AT procedure. Similarly, when all criteria are applied and only complete AT procedures (i.e., formulas 1–6) are considered, 27 of the 30 studies no longer qualify. The accumulation and description of a larger fund of well-controlled studies on AT is therefore crucial.

Review material was drawn from the bibliography of the Luthe and Schultz (1969) series on AT, from computer searches on the MEDLINE and the Psychological Abstracts system covering the English and German literature for the complete years 1969–1989, and from searches of secondary sources (i.e., references cited in papers identified with the first two search strategies). Results are presented and discussed separately for specific disorders and areas of application. Although earlier in this book a long list of areas of application for AT was described (primarily based on Schultz and Luthe's work [1969]), the areas of application reviewed in this chapter on controlled outcome studies are much shorter. Target behaviors/disorders covered include (in alphabetical order): angina pectoris, asthma, childbirth, essential hypertension, headaches (including migraines), hysteria, infertility, insomnia, rehabilitation from postmycardial infarction, Raynaud's disease, schizophrenia, tension reduction, and test anxiety. Key features of a given study (i.e., reference, design, size, AT procedure and outcome) are listed in table format (Table 6). Summary comments on the design quality and trustworthiness of findings, as well as on unresolved research questions, are provided in the text and accompany the information in the tables.

Angina Pectoris

Only one study (Laberke, 1952) could be found that used AT in a control group to treat angina. The fairly large and comparable (in terms of angina symptoms) samples and the 4-year follow-up make this a valuable study, and the choice of mycardial infarction morbidity as an endpoint further strengthens its clinical importance. None of the AT patients had an M.I. within 4 years, whereas four of the medicated patients did. Corroboration of this finding with a larger sample and more complex risk factor intervention packages would be most timely.

Asthma

Two studies were found (Deter & Allert, 1983; Spiess et al., 1988) and both report the usefulness of AT. However, it needs to be pointed out that neither paper clearly describes which AT procedures were used, nor was AT the only treatment component. In both studies AT was embedded in lengthy group therapy, which also involved discussions of the illness itself and coping attempts. In consequence, the effect of AT alone on asthma is not known. Because it would be unethical to provide a therapy other than the best available, it cannot be recommended here that one study AT as a single technique for asthma. The results from both studies above suggest that a combination therapy (possibly with the inclusion of medication) is best. Nevertheless, future researchers can deal with the issue in a crossover design by first providing the information-giving or AT component, testing its relative effectiveness, and then crossing patients over into the other treatment. Thus, specific training effects can be studied while maintaining ideal treatment conditions. The price to pay of course is the unavailability of follow-up information on the effectiveness of a single technique.

Childbirth

Although only one controlled study could be found in this category, Prill's (1965) work is particularly impressive. An unusually large sample was tested and the advantage of AT over no treatment for the reduction and length of labor pain is very convincing. AT-trained women had 30% shorter labor, 20% fewer contractions, and a subjectively less distressing birth experience. A slight variation of traditional AT was tested by Zimmermann-Tansella, et al. (1979) in primipara women. These authors compared a Lamaze-trained group with a group taught a method called "respiratory autogenic training." All subjects received 9 weeks of training, and the modified AT appears to have entailed the full standard AT package as well as some additional (but not clearly described) respiration exercises. The two methods were chosen for contrast because the AT procedure instructed the women to learn a regular,

Table 6: Controlled Clinical Outcome Studies Involving AT

Target problem/ behavior	Treatment groups	Treatment length and AT formulas used	Outcome	Follow-up
Angina pectoris	1. AT (N=31) 2. Medication control (N=30)	Laberke (1952) Length unspecified, standard formulas 1–6	Four of 30 patients in the medication group had myocardial infarctions within 4 years, none of the AT-trained individuals did	See outcome
Asthma	1. Information giving, illness discussion and AT (N=9) 2. Same as above but functional relaxation instead of AT (N=10) 3. No-treatment control (N=12)	Deter and Allert (1963) AT formulas not specified 50 sessions x 60 min.	Both active treatments reduced use of sympathomimetic and steroid medication, and showed decreased number of physician visits, no active treatment effect on pulmonological function was noted	Yes, but length was not specified
Asthma	Repeated treatment design Comparison 1: 1. Information giving (N=23) 2. Waiting-list control (N=18)	Spiess, Sachs, Buchinger, et al. (1988) 8 session x 90 min.	Treatment reduced trait anxiety perceived breathlessness, and insomnia. Treatment did not positively affect vital capacity or respiratory resistance	No

118

	Comparison 2 (patients drawn from information-giving group): 1. Additional AT (N=15) 2. No-AT control (N=8)	7 sessions x 90 min., formulas not specified	AT addition further reduced urge to cough, but neither vital capacity nor resistance improved	No
		Prill (1965)		
Childbirth	1. AT (N=104) 2. No-treatment control (N=300)	Formulas 1 and 2	AT reduced staff-rated labor pain, cervical dilation time (from 14.5 vs. 10.7 hrs.) and number of contractions (103 vs. 126)	Not applicable
		Zimmerman-Tansella et al. (1979)		
Childbirth	1. AT with additional respiration exercises 2. Lamaze-type birth preparation	9 weekly sessions, formulas not specified	AT reduced pre-labor anxiety and labor pain, and shortened expulsion time	Not applicable
		Juenet, Cottraux, & Collet (1983)		
Headache, tension	1. AT (N=15) 2. GSR biofeedback (N=16)	10 sessions x 40 min., formulas not specified	Headache frequency, headache intensity, and anxiety reduced in both treatments, GSR better for intensity reduction	6 months. Effect mostly maintained, no difference between groups

(cont.)

119

Table 6 (cont.)

Target problem/ behavior	Treatment groups	Treatment length and AT formulas used	Outcome	Follow-up
		Janssen & Neutgens (1986)		
Headache, tension (N=10) migraine (N=12) and combined (N=19)	1. AT	12 sessions x 60 min., standard formulas	At and PMR equally successful for migraine, PMR weaker than AT for combined headaches, only PMR effective for tension headache	3 months. AT and PMR still equally effective for migraine and combined headache, AT no effect on tension headache, PMR effects maintained
	2. Progressive muscular relax- ation (PMR)			
		Sargent, et al. (1986)		
Headache, migraine	1. No-treatment control (N=34)	22 sessions formulas not specified	All treatments were better than no treatment, EMG biofeedback was marginally better than either AT or temperature feedback, neither treatment affected medication usage	Unclear
	2. AT (N=34)			
	3. EMG biofeedback and and AT (N=34)			
	4. Temperature biofeedback and AT (N=34)			

Disorder	Treatment groups	Sessions	Results	Follow-up
Katzenstein, Kriegel, & Gaefke (1974)				
Hypertension	1. Cognitive therapy (N=46)	Approx. 25 sessions x 60 min., formulas not specified	-28/-19 SBP/DBP (mmHg)	2 years -13/-7
	2. Antihypertensive drug and AT (N=40)		-19/-13 SBP/DBP (mmHg)	-8/-5
	3. Antihypertensive drug and AT (N=14)		-19/-14 SBP/DBP (mmHg)	-4/-4
	4. Antihypertensive and psychopharmacological drug (N=21)		-21/-22 SBP/DBP (mmHg)	-13/-14
	5. Antihypertensive and psychopharmacological drug and AT (N=15)		-23/-13 SBP/DBP (mmHg)	-12/-12
Fray (1975)				
Hypertension	1. EMG biofeedback (N=10)	10 sessions, length unspecified	Both EMG and AT produced diastolic pressure reduction relative to no control (exact change in mmHg not available)	3 months. AT maintained training effects, EMG biofeedback did not
	2. AT (N=10)			
	3. No-treatment control (N=10)			
Luborsky, Ancona, Masoni, Scolari, & Longoni (1980–81)				
Hypertension	1. Pharmacological treatment (N=5)	Formulas 1, 2 and 4 9 sessions x 45 min.	-29.8/-24.8 mmHg SBP/DBP	2 weeks
	2. AT (N=5)		-7.0/-3.4 mmHg SBP/DBP	

(cont.)

Table 6 (cont.)

Target problem/ behavior	Treatment groups	Treatment length and AT formulas used	Outcome	Follow-up
	3. Combination of both above (N=5)		-6.2/-10.4 mmHg SBP/DBP	
Hypertension		Aivazyan, Zaitsev, Salenko, Yorenev, & Petrusheva (1988)		
	1. AT (N=23)	14–16 sessions x 50 min., AT procedure modified using visual symbol rather than standard formulas	At 6 weeks of treatment -8/–6 mmHg SBP/DBP	12 months -7/–6
	2. Thermal biofeedback (N=24)		–12/–9 mmHg SBP/DBP	–12/–9
	3. Breathing relaxation (N=23)		–10/–8mmHg SBP/DBP	–10/–8
	4. No-treatment control (N=24)		–2/–3 mmHg SBP/DBP	+1/–1
	5. Placebo control (N=24)		–4/–5 mmHg SBP/DBP	–3/–2
Hypertension 5-year follow-up		Aivazyan, Zaitsev, & Yurenev (1988)		
	1. AT (N=44)	6 months, procedure not specified	At 5-year follow-up 1. –5.8/–3.2 mmHg SBP/DBP	See Outcome
	2. No-behavioral-treatment control (N=46)		2. +4.3/+2.0 mmHg SBP/DBP Treated patients revealed less increase in left-ventricular cardiac mass (+14.6 g vs. +38.2 g) and fewer sick days	

Condition	Study / Groups	Results	Follow-up
Hypertension	Blanchard, et al. (1988) 1. AT (N=21) 20 sessions x 45 min., modified AT included visualization of relaxation figure 2. Thermal biofeedback (N=20) 3. Self-relaxation control (N=18)	1. −9.6/−7.6 mmHg SBP/DBP 2. −7.6/−9.5 mmHg SBP/DBP 3. −2.9/−3.7 mmHg SBP/DBP	12 months
Hypertension	Rossi, Caldari, Costa, & Ambrosiani (1989) AT in a within-subject placebo-controlled design 10 sessions x 90 min. standard formulas 1–6	Significant decrease of SBP −12.4 mmHg (over and above placebo effects) and a trend towards reduced DBP (−3.9 mmHg)	Approx. 2 months
Hysteria	Scallet, Cloninger, & Othmer (1976) 1. AT (N=5) 12 sessions x 40 min., formulas 1–6 2. AT and central electrosleep (N=5) 3. AT and peripheral electrosleep (N=7)	All groups showed improvement in mood but no reduction in somatic complaints	1 month. groups 2 and 3 relapsed but 1 maintained treatment gains
Infertility	O'Moore, O'Moore, Harrison, Murphy, & Carruthers (1983) 1. AT (N=13) 8 sessions x 60 min., standard formulas 2. Controls (N=10)	Infertile women were more anxious and tense and had higher prolactin levels than controls at pretest. AT reduced anxiety/tension and normalized prolactin levels. One AT-trained woman became pregnant during training.	No

(cont.)

Table 6 (cont.)

Target problem/behavior	Treatment groups	Treatment length and AT formulas used	Outcome	Follow-up
		Nicassio & Bootzin (1974)		
Insomnia	1. AT	Heaviness and warmth formulas only, 4 weeks	Both AT and PMR equally and effectively reduced time until falling asleep, pupillography and peer evaluation corroborated the findings	6 months (but incomplete). Training effects were maintained
	2. PMR			
	3. Self-relaxation			
	4. No-treatment control			
		Coursey, Frankel, Gaarder, & Mott (1980)		
Insomnia	1. AT (N=6)	12 sessions x 45 min., formulas 1–6	No improvement with electrosleep, 2 of 6 AT subjects and 3 of 6 EMG subjects improved on EEG sleep measures and self-report	1 month. Treatment gains were maintained
	2. Frontal EMG biofeedback (N=6)			
	3. Electrosleep (N=10)			
		Blackova, Bockova, & Sedivec (1982)		
Recovery from myocardial infarction	1. AT (N=131) and standard internist care	32 sessions, standard formulas	AT reduced anxiety, neuroticism, depression, fatigue, and resting rate heart	No
	2. Controls (N=48) standard internist care only			

124

Population	Treatment	Study / Sessions	Results	Follow-up
Raynaud's disease (N=30 at post-treatment; N=19 at 1-year follow-up)	1a. AT, full training 1b. AT, short training 2a. AT and temperature biofeedback, full 2b. AT and temperature biofeedback, short training	Keefe, Surwit, & Pilon (1979) 6 sessions, —1a and 2a, 2 sessions, —1b and 2b, formulas 1 and 2 only	All treatment led to decrease in vasospastive attacks, and permitted digital temperature control in the lab	1 year. Maintenance of 50% reduction in frequency of vasospastic attacks; loss of ability to maintain digital temperature increases in lab
Raynaud's disease	1. AT (N=7) 2. AT and temperature biofeedback (N=7)	Surwit & Fenton (1980) 6 sessions x 45 min., formulas 1 and 2 only	Both treatments produced increases in skin temperature, However AT with biofeedback was superior in outcome	No
Raynaud's disease	1. AT 2. PMR 3. Autogenic biofeedback	Keefe, Surwit, & Pilon (1980) 3 sessions x 60 min., formulas 1 and 2 only	All treatment led to decrease in vasospastive attacks and permitted digital temperature control in the lab, no group differences emerged	

(cont.)

Table 6 (cont.)

Target problem/ behavior	Treatment groups	Treatment length and AT formulas used	Outcome	Follow-up
Raynaud's disease	1. Temperature biofeedback (N=8)	Freedman, Ianni, & Waring (1983) 10 bi-weekly sessions, formulas 1 and 2 only	Temperature biofeedback was better than EMG biofeedback or AT; temperature feedback during cold stress was best	1 year. Addition of cold stress training improved biofeedback effects, decreases in symptom reports were −93% for 2, −69% for 1, −33% for 4, and −17% for 3
	2. As for 1 but under cold stress (N=8)			
	3. Frontalis EMG biofeedback (N=8)			
	4. AT (N=8)			
Schizophrenia	1. AT (N=15)	Motoda, Shibata, Inanaga, & Isozaki (1969) 3 months, standard formulas	EEG visual-evoked responses are stabilized with AT relative to controls	Not available
	2. No-treatment control (N=12)			
Stress, anxiety, and tension	1. AT (N=8)	Hartman (1982) 3 sessions x 60 min. formulas 1 and 2 only	Cognitive and somatic anxiety was reduced with training, AT	3 weeks

126

Focus	Study	Treatment groups	Design	Results	Follow-up
		2. PMR (N=8)		and PMR did not differ significantly	
Stress, anxiety, and tension (self-perceived)	Herbert & Gutmann (1983)	1. AT (N=62) 2. No-treatment controls (N=10)	6 sessions x 90 min., standard formulas	State and trait anxiety were reduced by AT	6 weeks. Anxiety reduction maintained
Stress, anxiety, and tension (self-perceived)	Banner & Meadows (1983)	1. EMG feedback (N=11) 2. Finger temperature feedback (N=12) 3. 1 and 2 combined (N=12) 4. AT (N=9) 5. Placebo control (N=9) 6. Waiting-list control (N=10)	9 sessions x 60 min., tape-recorded and modified	All groups showed equal reduction of tension and anxiety (subjectively) but no physiological change (EMG or finger temperature) occurred	3 months
Test anxiety	Reed & Meyer (1974)	1. "Passive" AT 2. "Active" AT	3 sessions, formulas 1 and 2 only	AT reduced test anxiety and increased perceived relaxation, no group differences	Not available
Test anxiety	Sellers (1974)	1. AT, taught individually 2. AT in groups	Length not specified, formulas 1 and 2 only	AT reduced test anxiety, no group differences in outcome	Not available

relaxed form of breathing, whereas the Lamaze method more specifically prepared the women for the deep and forced respiration used during labor. On many birth outcome and process variables both groups were similar, but the AT-trained women reported less anxiety prior to labor and less pain during labor. Furthermore, the expulsion time was shorter for the AT group, thus replicating Prill's (1965) observations. Based on these findings the use of AT for birth preparation appears highly recommendable.

Essential Hypertension

The efficacy of AT for hypertension has already been reported by Luthe (1963). Luthe's data are particularly difficult to interpret because mean changes are not reported (only the percentage improved) and no control-group data are available. Lantzsch and Drunkenmoelle (1975) also provided interesting data on the specific acute effects of AT for hypertensives. They conducted a comprehensive cardiac evaluation in 10 hypertensives and 10 normotensive controls. The first and second AT formulas (warmth and heaviness) were found to trigger acute reductions of stroke volume in hypertensives (–20%) but increases in normotensives, while mean arterial pressure decreased in hypertensives but remained unchanged in the controls, and heart rate was stable in both groups. These findings suggest that AT may provoke autonomic self-regulation in the desired direction. However interesting these findings are, though, none of these studies were controlled group studies with clear descriptions of outcome.

The literature search conducted for this book revealed seven studies on hypertension with controlled experimental designs. The majority of these (and also the better designed ones) have appeared in 1988 and 1989. Of all the studies that used some form of AT as a single therapy, only Luborksy, Ancona, Masoni, Scolari, and Langoni (1980–1981) failed to-report significant AT-induced reductions in blood pressure. Their samples, however, are also the smallest (N = 5) and their observed change was quite similar to the changes observed in the other studies. Overall, it appears that systolic pressure is more effectively reduced with AT than is diastolic pressure, with the change magnitudes tending to be smaller than with drug therapy. Katzenstein, Kriegel, and Gaefke's study (1974) is the largest and provides promising data on the acute and long-term effectiveness of a psychological treatment package that includes AT and a cognitive–behavioral intervention. The impact of this treatment matched and in some comparisons exceeded the effect of pharmacological therapy both in acute treatment response as well as in the 2-year follow-up data. Unfortunately this paper is extremely short given the richness of the researchers' efforts and the therapy results are presented in a cryptic manner. Change scores as presented in Table 6, for example, had to be extracted through extrapolation from a graphic display in their paper. The data suggest that adding AT to drug therapy had no additional effect over drug treatment alone. This is also consistent with Luborsky et al.'s (1980–1981) findings.

The contrasting of AT with other behavioral relaxation techniques also produces a somewhat uneven picture. Fray (1975) finds AT comparable to muscle tension feedback at the end of treatment but superior at 3-month follow-up. Blanchard et al. (1988) report equal change for AT and thermal biofeedback, but Aivazyan, Zaitsev, Salenko, Yurenev, & Patrusheva (1988) observed slightly more change with thermal biofeedback and breathing relaxation than with AT. As a whole, it would appear that previous conclusions on the overall equal effectiveness of different relaxation procedures for hypertension are still justified (Benson, 1975; Linden, 1984).

Three of the studies described here stem from a joint USA–USSR symposium on hypertension research and are published in a supplement to the journal *Health Psychology* (Blanchard et al., 1988; Aivazyan, Zaitsev, Salenko, Yurenev, & Petru-

sheva 1988). Taken together these three articles provide a rich
fund of treatment observations, with implications for the consideration of baseline differences on blood pressure reduction,
differentiating significant change from clinically relevant
change, and the matching of technique to patient. The study
described by Blanchard et al. (1988) was a joint study for which
half of the data were collected in the USSR and the other half in
the USA using identical procedures. Interesting differences
emerged. The Soviet patients started with higher systolic pressure levels and also showed greater systolic decreases thus
confirming Jacob, Kraemer, and Agras's (1977) findings that
higher levels of pretreatment pressure also predicted greater
treatment responses. Soviet patients also showed a better maintenance of treatment effects, and at a 12-month follow-up 75%
of the Soviet patients had diastolic pressures below 90 mmHg
(i.e., considered controlled) whereas only 24% of the American
patients fell below 90 mmHg diastolic. The authors interpreted
these differences as reflecting different levels of motivation
leading to differential compliance, possibly mediated by differ-
ing perspectives on the credibility of these treatments.

One potential weakness of studies on blood pressure reduction is that office-measured pressures may not accurately
reflect real-life blood pressure levels and, hence, may possess
questionable validity. Current attempts to deal with this problem are based on 24-hour ambulatory monitoring and have already revealed the superiority of this method for blood
pressure prognosis (Perloff, Sokolow, & Cowan, 1983). Unfortunately no study using AT for hypertension has also reported
ambulatory effects. This absence of such information is somewhat balanced by Aivazyan, Zaitsev, & Yurenev's (1988b) data
on other clinical endpoints over a 5-year observation period.
That is, AT-trained patients showed significantly less increase
in left ventricular mass and took less sick days than their untreated cohorts. The observation of the maintenance of initial
treatment effects up to 5 years is impressive and clearly sup-

ports the usefulness of AT. Further, Aivazyan (1988b) produced very convincing data that those patients who continued to practice AT showed superior maintenance to their less compliant peers: the relative changes over 5 years were −13.2 mmHg SBP and −5.8 mmHg DBP for the continued users, in comparison to +4.9 mmHg SBP and +1.9 mmHg DBP for the nonusers of AT. A breakdown of the mean changes due to behavioral therapy also revealed that in the treated group 32% improved, 59% remained unchanged, and 9% deteriorated over 5 years whereas in the control group 59% also remained unchanged, 11% improved even without therapy but 30% deteriorated. These figures clearly illustrate that statistically significant mean changes hide great variability, that few patients can be considered true responders, and that one of the main effects of AT (or other treatments) is the prevention of deterioration. Also, it is clear that the identification of which patient will benefit most from AT promises increased cost-effectiveness.

Although it was impressive to see that a considerable number of controlled studies of sufficient treatment length were available to judge the effectiveness of AT's blood pressure reducing propensity, it is unfortunate that these studies also had considerable variations in the AT procedures used. The basic autogenic principle is supported by the above findings but whether and, if so, how AT protocol variations may impact on the outcome for hypertension treatment remains unknown.

Headaches

Three controlled studies could be found on AT and headaches: Juenet, Cottraux, and Collet (1983), Janssen and Neutgens (1986), and Sargent et al. (1986). All of these studies possessed strong control group designs, reasonable treatment lengths, and provided coherent pictures of the outcomes of AT for headaches. As a whole, AT was effective in reducing headache frequency and intensity, and training effects were found to be maintained at follow-up. Adding autogenic phrases to EMG or temperature biofeedback (Sargent et al., 1986) had no additional effects over AT alone. At the end of acute treatment GSR biofeedback was superior to AT, but this difference disappears at follow-up (Juenet at al., 1983). The Janssen and Neutgens study (1986) is also important because tension headache, migraines, and mixed headache groups are compared and two different relaxation treatments—AT and muscular relaxation—are offered. Although both relaxation procedures are presumed to trigger the same relaxation response (which in turn is presumed to account for the treatment effect), treatment outcome was highly specific and differential for various problem-technique combinations. AT was of no use for tension headache patients, but was clearly effective for migraines and the combined headache types.

The three studies, when evaluated jointly, indicate that AT should not be the treatment of choice for tension headache (GSR or other biofeedback may be superior), but that it is clearly indicated with migraine and mixed headaches. Janssen and Neutgens' (1986) observations of highly specific treatment effects support the original claim (see Chapter 12 on research supporting autogenic principles) that AT may trigger autonomically specific changes that other relaxation procedures may not provoke. The overall good quality of the designs used to evaluate AT and headaches, and the fairly large sample sizes enhance the trustworthiness and generalizability of these findings. Janssen and Neutgens' findings also highlight how much change clinicians and patients can expect with AT. A combination intensity X duration score revealed a 40% reduction in headache severity for both the migraine and mixed headache types at follow-up, but AT was also associated with an approximately 20% increase in headache severity for AT-treated patients with tension headaches.

Hysteria

Chronic hysteria (now termed Histrionic Personality Disorder in psychiatric classification systems) was the target of AT treatment described by Scallet, Cloninger, and Othmer (1976). No particular rationale for choosing AT was provided. The control treatment was electrosleep with either peripheral or central electrode placement, which was also added to the basic AT procedure. Electrosleep was described as a nonconvulsive, electrical stimulation of the brain. Noticeable treatment effects were reported at the end of treatment for all groups but only in terms of their effect on depression. AT relaxation without electrosleep was the only method that had maintained a positive outcome at follow-up.

Given the lack of a clear rationale for using AT with histrionic patients and the weak findings reported here, it is not surprising that no further studies using AT for this disorder could be found.

Infertility

A conference paper by Sakakura, Iwabuchi, and Murata (1967) provided some encouraging data on AT for infertility. Eight of 22 infertile women treated with AT became pregnant within 12 months and another five at a later time. Unfortunately, no control group data were reported and the design of the study was not clearly spelled out. More convincing are the findings of O'Moore, O'Moore, Harrison, Murphy, and Carruthers (1983) who investigated AT effects in 13 infertile couples (mean length of infertility 6.7 years) and 10 control couples. The group differences at pretreatment and in training effects are noteworthy. The patient sample was psychologically different from the controls at baseline in that high anxiety and guilt-proneness were reported, and the patients also exhibited high levels of prolactin. By the end of treatment, anxiety had decreased, as had the prolactin levels, which approached normal values. These data support arguments that infertility may be stress-related and that AT may serve to reduce stress at the subjective level as well as with respect to critical biological indices. One infertile woman became pregnant during therapy, but unfortunately no outcome beyond active AT therapy is reported. No information on the critical post-therapy months was provided, which is most unfortunate since the treatment effectiveness for this particular clinical application must be tested over a lengthy posttreatment period. Infertility appears to be an area where AT holds promise, but a convincing demonstration of its value is left to future research.

Insomnia

Two controlled studies on AT for insomnia were available (Nicassio & Bootzin, 1974; Coursey, Frankel, Gaarder, & Mott, 1980). Kahn, Weiss, and Baker (1968) had earlier reported that only two weeks of AT were sufficient to trigger improvement in insomnia, although this treatment cannot be aptly called AT since training success in achieving AT sensations requires longer practice (Mensen, 1975). Kahn et al. (1968) also had no control group. Nicassio and Bootzin improved on this design by providing four weeks of training (heaviness and warmth formulas only) and randomly assigning 30 insomniacs to either muscular relaxation, AT, self-relaxation, or no-treatment control. All active therapy worked and improvement was noted on self-reports of progress, peer evaluations, and in-laboratory pupillography. A 6-month follow-up confirmed the findings. Coursey et al. (1980) also reported similar improvement for two different relaxation conditions (AT and muscular relaxation), but demonstrated that clinical success as apparent in mean group changes was evident in only half of the treated patients. No prediction of treatment failures on the basis of psychological features could be made.

Recovery from Myocardial Infarction

Because behavioral and emotional factors are important in the post M.I. recovery process and because their modification improves the prognosis of these patients (Friedman et al., 1986), AT with its stress-reducing propensities is worth testing. Polacková, Bocková, and Sedivec (1982) trained 131 post M.I. patients in AT and compared them to 48 controls. Although psychological factors (anxiety, neuroticism, depression, and fatigue) and heart rate levels improved with AT, recurrent infarction rates (which would be the most crucial outcome variable) were not reported in this study. Hence, the findings suggest that AT-triggered stress reduction did take place, but its potential preventive effect on M.I. recurrence has not been demonstrated.

Raynaud's Disease

Four controlled studies could be identified (Keefe, 1978; Keefe, Surwit, & Pilon, 1979, 1980; Surwit, Pilon, & Fenton, 1978; Freedman, Ianni, & Wenig, 1983). All of these confirm the positive treatment effects of AT when compared to baseline or no-treatment control conditions. Follow-up investigations also supported the maintenance of initial training effects with AT. The most recent of these studies with the most sophisticated design (Freedman et al., 1983) also suggests that temperature feedback is more effective than AT, and that temperature biofeedback executed during cold stress is clearly the most powerful behavioral treatment known at this time. This was true at the end of training as well as at a 1-year follow-up. The design quality of these studies is generally good, but it must be pointed out that none of these studies applied standardized AT with the 6 formulas and extensive training. All used the warmth and heaviness formulas only, relied on taped instructions, and provided minimal training. This criticism does not detract from the observation of clinical improvement in Raynaud's symptoms with abbreviated AT, but it must be highlighted that full-length AT has never been applied to Raynaud's patient in a controlled study and its overall and comparative efficacy remains to be determined. Because the impact of biofeedback on Raynaud's symptoms was significantly enhanced by providing the training during a cold challenge, it would be most interesting to compare AT and biofeedback when both are taught during the appropriate cold challenges. The findings of Polzien (1955) on AT effects on skin temperature when practiced in a cold room also provide experimental support for the promise of teaching AT during cold challenge to Raynaud's patients.

Schizophrenia

Motoda, Shibata, Inanga, and Isozaki (1969) reported the only known controlled application of AT to schizophrenic patients. Whereas the clinical endpoint of visually evoked responses can be considered a valuable hard criterion for positive AT outcome, additional outcome data like comparison with other treatments, medication needs, and long-term behavioral changes would have been most useful. Also, if researchers intend to continue in this vein, more basic research supporting the rationale of using AT for schizophrenia is needed.

Self-perceived Stress, Anxiety, and Tension

Many stress-related disorders frequently come to the attention of the physician and/or clinical psychologist under the guise of vague, undefined symptoms. Rather than classifying each patient first and then offering stress management programs, Herbert and Gutman (1983) evaluated AT in its most cost-effective application—that is, group training with a preventive perspective, for those patients who perceive themselves as stressed. Pre-treatment anxiety levels were clearly elevated and approached normal levels after full-length AT, whereas controls remained unchanged. A most valuable extension of this strategy would be to train a large number of similar patients with AT and then follow-up their health service use relative to that of untrained patients. This strategy would also permit a cost–benefit evaluation and thus strengthen the objective of prevention which underlied the Herbert and Gutman (1983) study.

Banner and Meadows (1983) targeted a similar population with the intent of identifying treatment technique specificity. These researchers offered a variety of treatments (including biofeedback, AT, placebo, and wait-list controls) and chose subjective as well as physiological resting and reactivity indices as their dependent variables. All groups improved equally, thus pointing out the placebo-based effects of any psychological approach including that of simply waiting for treatment. These findings present a challenge to go beyond the mere testing of a technique and instead to deal with patient–problem–technique matching for optimal outcome.

Test Anxiety

Two controlled studies were identified (see also Table 6): Reed and Meyer (1974) and Sellers (1974). Both studies applied brief treatments with the heaviness and warmth formulas only, and neither one had a no-treatment or placebo control. Both were successful on subjective measures of anxiety. Because of these design features, these studies support the utility of AT, without however offering much experimental control. The more interesting features, nonetheless, were the comparison of group versus individual training (Sellers, 1974) and the distinction of "active" versus "passive" AT (Reed & Meyer, 1974). AT was defined as "passive" when the standard instruction to "let it happen" was given, whereas "active" was defined as an in-

struction to "make the autogenic sensation happen." Neither
the group/individual distinction nor the active/passive dimen-
sion had significant impact on the outcome. How full-length
AT compares with the results reported here remains to be determined. Also, how full-length AT would compare with other
promising approaches to treating test anxiety like cognitive restructuring (Dobson, 1988) needs to be tested.

Summary of Outcome Findings

This review of the outcome literature, which focused on controlled therapy studies, adds much needed support to the ac-
claimed potential of AT as a treatment for psychological/psy-
chosomatic dysfunctions and applications. With the exception
of one study on tension headache (where AT was found to actually worsen the outcome), AT was consistently effective in
promoting improvement relative to baseline conditions, was
more effective than a placebo, and more effective than no
treatment or minimal treatment control (with exception of the
Banner and Meadows study [1983] where everybody improved). AT was not as effective as Progressive Muscular Relaxation for treating tension headaches (Janssen & Neutgens,
1986) or as effective as thermal biofeedback during cold stress
for the treatment of Raynaud's disease, and so in these two instances AT appears contraindicated, as other behavioral methods were demonstrated to be better. On the other hand, AT
was better for medication control for angina and rehabilitation
from myocardial infarction, better than EMG biofeedback for
mixed headaches, and better than EMG biofeedback for hypertension. Inconsistent findings were noted only for tension
headache, where AT was superior to electrodermal feedback
but worse than Progressive Muscular Relaxation.

Procedural variations (i.e., short versus long training, individual versus group training, and instruction to achieve relaxation passively versus actively) had no discernible effects on the

outcome. However, these comparisons were executed only within studies on test anxiety or Raynaud's disease (for the long versus short training comparison) and in all these studies reduced-length AT (formulas 1 and 2 only) had been provided.

AT outcome when related to specific areas of application was particularly strong for the treatment of cardiovascular problems (hypertension, angina, myocardial infarction rehabilitation), facilitation of childbirth, and to a lesser degree for the treatment of migraines. In other areas of application AT was consistently associated with improvement over baselines, no treatment, or minimal treatment controls, but was generally equivalent to other behavioral treatments like Progressive Muscular Relaxation or biofeedback. In summary, it appears that AT is generally as effective as other behavioral treatments, but instances can be identified where it is worse than other treatments (tension headaches) and hence not indicated, or better than other treatments, and therefore should be prescribed. Because of this noted specificity in AT outcome, it is not recommended to consider AT a universal treatment that is always exchangeable with other behavioral methods.

As a result of the sampling of German- as well as English-language publications, the use of specific criteria for determining a controlled study, and the inclusion of recent studies, the current review partially overlaps but also adds many new observations to Pikoff's (1984) earlier conclusions. Because of differences in the reviewing methods, more than half of the studies reviewed by Pikoff are not included here, but 17 different studies (more recent ones or those published in German) are now included. In comparing Pikoff's study with the findings here, the following picture emerges: no new, controlled studies using AT were found for insomnia, hysteria, or test anxiety. The literature on hypertension now provides a much richer and more promising picture for the use of AT. Supportive findings on AT for angina pectoris, asthma, childbirth, infertility, and recovery from mycardial infarction are novel to this review. Thus, the current review adds considerable

strength to Pikoff's observations on the clinical usefulness of
AT. Further, many of the studies mentioned here for the first
time tend to have more adequate treatment lengths and better
experimental designs. It was intriguing to note that North
American researchers frequently modified or abbreviated AT
without testing its comparability to the original, full-length
method whereas German-language researchers typically used
the complete procedure. This observation confirms Pikoff's
conclusion that "taking such liberties with the original technique means, in effect, that AT per se has not really been
tested experimentally in this country" (i.e., in the United
States). Fortunately, the current review concludes that more
appropriate studies for the evaluation of AT are now available,
especially when research in German and that which was published since Pikoff's review are also considered.

⋄14⋄

Review of Outcome for Nonclinical Applications

Although Luthe (Volume III, 1969b) reported a long list of apparently successful nonclinical applications, only three controlled studies could be found that qualify for review in this chapter. The earliest study deals with performance anxiety and flight performance in pilot trainees (Barton, 1981), whereas the later two studies deal with motion sickness in space and other aviation applications (Cowings & Toscano, 1982; Toscano & Cowings, 1982).

Barton (1981) randomly assigned eight pilot trainees to each of three conditions: (1) no intervention control, (2) EMG biofeedback, and (3) an audiotaped presentation of the heaviness and warmth formulas from AT. Training consisted of six sessions respectively and dependent variables were state and trait anxiety, EMG levels and heart rate, as well as two flight performance variables (timing and flight accuracy). None of the conditions affected flight performance, but both active treatments reduced state anxiety and EMG levels. Biofeedback was found superior to the abbreviated AT.

In the first of the motion sickness studies (Toscano & Cowings, 1982), eighteen men were randomly assigned to either autogenic training (six sessions, standard formulas), a cognitive control task, or a no-treatment control. Neither those in the control task condition nor those in the no-treatment condition showed any change in their ability to tolerate rotation, whereas the AT-trained group tolerated approximately five times more rotation before reaching the motion sickness threshold. The absence of a treatment effect for the cognitive control task was interpreted as supporting the notion of AT effect specificity, thus ruling out simple distraction as an explanation. Cowings and Toscano (1982) next replicated the findings with 24 men who were chosen to reflect high to moderate motion sickness susceptibility groups. Half of the subjects were left untreated, while the remainder received the same AT package as the first study. Both untreated groups did not change, but both treated groups responded as well as had been demonstrated in the first study. The highly susceptible subjects did not reach the same level of improvement as the moderately susceptible ones, however their baseline scores had also been lower and the improvement slopes were comparable in both groups. Relative to other studies on AT outcome, these three studies represent consistently strong designs with good experimental control, random assignment, and multiple measures. The series of studies by Toscano and Cowings is furthermore impressive because of the replicated findings. Research of this quality makes a most valuable contribution to the literature on nonclinical uses of AT.

Part IV
Concluding Notes

The reader is now able to judge how well the objectives of this book as laid out in the introduction have been achieved. The clinical manual section was designed to give enough detail to permit the learning of AT without formal additional training. The research section was designed to provide the necessary empirical justification for clinical applications of AT, and also to highlight where trustworthy findings are available. By implication, this section also describes the many aspects of AT practice and application where much more research is indicated. Some of the key recommendations for clinical practice will be summarized here, and pertinent research questions to be tackled in future studies are similarly highlighted.

⬧ 15 ⬧

Recommendations for the Clinical Practice of AT

Integration of the research findings with the suggestions for clinical practice made in the manual section indicate the need to stress a number of clinical practice features in this concluding section. I want to emphasize again that teaching AT to a patient makes little sense when the therapist has no experience with AT him- or herself. He or she will not be a credible therapist, may misread symptoms of discomfort, and is much more likely to lack the enthusiasm necessary to trigger optimism and enhance the necessary compliance in the trainee. Until research evidence (which is not yet available) suggests that abbreviated AT procedures are equally potent to produce clinically meaningful change, the practitioner is urged to teach the full AT procedure as laid out in this book (see the Appendix for a quick reference of a standard 8-week program). Throughout this book, and in other texts dealing with stress management procedures, authors have been able to

145

show repeatedly that relaxation procedures are not as effective when taught via tape as when integrated into a therapeutic relationship. Given our knowledge base and beliefs about what psychotherapy is and why it works, and considering the demonstrated impact of nonspecific factors in psychotherapy (Shapiro & Shapiro, 1982), this is not surprising. Whether AT is best taught in groups or individually is empirically unresolved, but the advantages of each method of presentation are obvious and the decision for group or individual training is best made by clinical common sense. Also, I want to stress again that learning and teaching AT without any background in psychological therapy is at least unwise, and possibly could cause harm to patients.

Recommendations for Future Research

This book and its predecessors (i.e., the Luthe and Schultz series, 1969–1970) have been able to refer to a remarkably large body of background literature on AT. The wealth of available information, however, needs to be critically screened to highlight the more trustworthy research findings. Design flaws in and difficult access to some reported findings are the most likely culprits for our not having an even stronger research base. Many of these methodological flaws are avoidable, however, and recommendations for improvement are made here.

Having read both the German and English literatures on AT, very distinct research and publication patterns emerged. German researchers hardly ever abbreviated the standard AT procedure and were more likely to apply AT to clinical samples. Unfortunately they also had a tendency to report their findings in conference proceedings or books that are not widely read, and they frequently presented incomplete reports of their findings, thereby making replications difficult. English-language researchers have taken considerable liberty with the AT procedure and have predominantly applied abbreviated procedures, often to analog populations. The reported findings, on the other hand, tend to appear in widely read journals, and are generally described in good detail. The reader looking for research supporting AT is often left unsatisfied. The studies that promise the most are not easy to access and are not well described, while the sources that are ready to access and the reports that are well described may lack the power to detect clinical effects.

Many recommendations arise from these observations and other findings described in the research section.

1. Researchers need to apply the full AT procedure and avoid taped instructions if maximal effects are to be obtained.

2. Home practice is essential for acquiring the autogenic "skill" and needs to be encouraged, controlled, and closely monitored in clinical outcome studies. Findings from a variety of different studies have shown that trainees who do not achieve the subjective autogenic sensations also fail to show the desired physiological changes. These patients may need to be excluded or studied separately from the successful trainees in outcome studies. Inclusion of noncompliant trainees in therapy groups will similarly water down the potentially demonstrable effect of any procedure and will make study outcomes unnecessarily conservative (Haynes & Dantes, 1987).

3. Because patient personality and therapy technique may need to be matched for best clinical outcome (see Chapter 10 above), the usual clinical design with complete random assignment to treatment conditions may be flawed if maximal clinical benefit is to be demonstrated. Random assignment can wipe out or weaken the potential of optimal patient–method matches.

Because there is good evidence that combinations of therapeutic methods (i.e., treatment packages as described above) are more effective than applications of single techniques (Shapiro & Shapiro, 1982), researchers may want to concentrate more on evaluations of method packages including an AT component for their clinical work and clinical research. Once the treatment package approach is implemented researchers can then attempt treatment-dismantling strategies by comparing the full package against a more limited package (Agras, Kazdin, & Wilson, 1979). By these means, one could identify the additional contribution that AT can make to a treatment package and/or identify other treatment techniques that are particularly complementary to AT.

At this time I see no need for further publications of single-case studies with AT unless a highly original clinical problem or application can be reported. The current need is for controlled studies with clinical populations and well-designed studies on the mechanisms of AT in action. Such studies need to be described in sufficient detail so that replication will be easy. The majority of successful single-patient clinical applications have not yet been subjected to controlled research. Nevertheless, a comparison of the outcome studies reported here with those reviewed by Pikoff (1984) reveals a strong case for the clinical usefulness of AT for a wide variety of disorders. Similarly, there is strong evidence for the comparable effectiveness of AT with other biobehavioral treatments, demonstrations of the unique strengths of AT (i.e., particularly in the domain of cardiovascular disease), as well as for its apparent weaknesses (i.e., for the case of tension headaches).

With respect to presumed mechanisms of action, a concluding note is called for as well. AT's presumed potential to achieve bidirectional change has been demonstrated (e.g., blood pressure reduction and increased peripheral blood flow). The research reviewed in this book primarily targets the reduction of central nervous system arousal and sympathetic activation. It does not systematically investigate the sympathetic/parasympathetic "balancing act" that is characteristic of the underlying homeostatic model of autonomic self-regulation.

In the same vein, a research strategy suggested by Lichstein (1988) deserves repeating here. Because of the difficulty in differentiating generalized from specific formula effects in AT, he suggested that clinicians train different groups with different orders of formulas. For example, a four-group design could be proposed where all groups receive training in one formula only (either warmth, heaviness, respiration, or heart) and are monitored in a pre–post format for 2–4 weeks. Measures pertinent to all potential effects (i.e., to muscle tension, vasodilation, heart rate, or full ECG) and respiratory indices (rate, expiration–inspiration length, amplitude) could be applied to all groups to test for specificity versus generality of effects. Furthermore, measures can be obtained at resting levels to measure long-term changes as well as during AT practice to detect acute effects. Next, subjects would receive the complete training in a crossover format, so that single-formula training results could finally be compared with full-package results.

Although much work remains to be done, the available literature has a great deal to offer toward strengthening the reputation that I firmly believe AT deserves. It is my hope that researchers and clinicians alike will be encouraged to carry on and expand their practice and investigations of Schultz's autogenic training for clinical and nonclinical applications. This will serve to enhance the quality of life for many patients for whom AT is not currently available.

References

Agras, W. S., Kazdin, A. E., & Wilson, G. T. (1979). *Behavior therapy: Toward an applied clinical science.* San Francisco: W.H. Freeman.

Aivazyan, T. A., Zaitsev, V. P., Salenko, B. B., Yurenev, A. P., & Patrusheva, I. F. (1988). Efficacy of relaxation techniques in hypertensive patients. *Health Psychology, 7(Suppl.),* 193–200.

Aivazyan, T. A., Zaitsev, V. P., & Yurenev, A. P. (1988). Autogenic training in the treatment and secondary prevention of essential hypertension: Five-year follow-up. *Health Psychology, 7(Suppl.),* 201–208.

Alnaes, R. (1966). Das Verhalten des Cortisols unter Hypnose oder Autogenem Training mit besonderer Beruecksichtigung der hypnosuggestiven Analgesie. *Psychotherapie und Psychosomatik, 14,* 395–397.

Aya, Y. (1967). Studies on the influence of emotions upon the blood cholesterol level. *Fukuoka Acta Medica, 58,* 7.

Badura, H. O. (1977). Beitrag zur differentialdiagnostischen Validitaet des MMPI zur Prognose der Effizienz des Autogenen Trainings. *Archiv fuer Psychiatrie und Nervenkrankheiten, 224,* 389–394.

Bandura, A. (1977). Self-efficacy: Toward a unifying theory of behavioral change. *Psychological Review, 84,* 191–215.

Banner, C. N., & Meadows, W. M. (1983). Examination of the effectiveness of various treatment techniques for reducing tension. *British Journal of Clinical Psychology, 22,* 183–193.

Barber, T. X. (1984). Hypnosis, deep relaxation, and active relaxation: Data, theory, and clinical applications. In Woolfolk, R. L. & Lehrer, P. M. (Eds.), *Principles and practice of stress management* (pp. 142–187). New York: Guilford Press.

Barton, J. W. (1981). *The effects of EMG biofeedback and autogenic train-ing on anxiety control and performance of aviation pilots.* Unpub-lished doctoral disseration, University of Alberta, Edmonton.

Benson, H. (1975). *The relaxation response.* New York: Morrow.

Bernstein, D. A., & Borkovec, T. D. (1973). *Progressive relaxation train-ing: A manual for the helping professions.* Champaign, IL: Research Press.

Blanchard, E. B., Khramelashvili, V. V., McCoy, G. C., Aivazyan, T. A., McCaffrey, R. J., Salenko, B. B., Musso, A., Wittrock, D. A., Berger, M., Gerardi, M. A., & Pangburn, L. (1988). The USA–USSR collaborative cross-cultural comparison of autogenic training and thermal biofeedback in the treatment of mild hy-pertension. *Health Psychology, 7(Suppl.),* 175–192.

Blizard, D. A., Cowings, P., & Miller, N. E. (1975). Visceral responses to opposite types of autogenic-training imagery. *Biological Psy-chology, 3,* 49–55.

Borkovec, T. D., & Fowles, D. C. (1973) Controlled investigation of the effects of progressive and hypnotic relaxation on insomnia. *Journal of Abnormal Psychology, 82,* 153–158.

Braud, W., & Masters, D. (1980). Electrodermal reactions to opposite types of autogenic training imagery. *Biological Psychology, 10,* 211–218.

Budzynski, T. H., Stoyva, J. M., & Pfeffer, K. E. (1980). Biofeedback techniques in psychosomatic disorders. In A. Goldstein & E. B. Foa (Eds.), *Handbook of behavioral interventions.* New York: Wiley.

Cannon, W. B. (1933). *The wisdom of the body.* New York: Norton.

Carruthers, M. (1979). Autogenic training. *Journal of Psychosomatic Research, 23,* 437–440.

Coursey, R. D., Frankel, B. L., Gaarder, K. R., & Mott, D. E. (1980). A comparison of relaxation techniques with electrosleep therapy for chronic sleep-onset insomnia. *Biofeedback and Self-Regulation, 5,* 57–73.

Cowings, P. S., & Toscano, W. B. (1982). The relationship of motion sickness susceptibility to learned autonomic control for symptom suppression. *Aviation, Space and Environmental Medicine, 53,* 570–575.

Davis, M., Robbins Eshelman, E., & McKay, M. (1982). *The relaxation and stress reduction workbook.* Oakland, CA: New Harbinger Publi-cations.

Deter, H. C., & Allert, G. (1983). Group therapy for asthma patients: A concept for the psychosomatic treatment of patients in a medi-cal clinic—A controlled study. *Psychotherapy and Psychosomatics, 40,* 95–105.

Dienstbier, R. A., (1989). Arousal and physiological toughness: Implications for mental and physical health. *Psychological Review, 96,* 84–100.

Dobeta, H., Sugano, H., & Ohno, Y. (1966). Circulatory changes during autogenic training. In J. J. Lopez Ibor, (Ed.), *IV World Congress of Psychiatry, Madrid* (International Congress Series, No. 117), Amsterdam: Excerpta Medica Foundation.

Dobson, K. S. (Ed.). (1988). *Handbook of cognitive–behavioral therapies.* New York: Guilford Press.

Dongier, S., DeGosseley, M., Roussenu, J. C., & Timsit-Berthier, M. (1967). Le training autogène et les potentiels évoqués par la stimulation sonore. *Revue de la Médicine Psychosomatique, 9,* 143–147.

Erickson, M. H., & Rossi, E. L. (1979). *Hypnotherapy: An exploratory casebook.* New York: Irvington.

Fahrion, S. L. (1978). Autogenic biofeedback treatment for migraine. *Research in Clinical Studies of Headache, 5,* 47–71.

Fischel, W., & Mueller, V. P. (1962). Psychogalvanische Hautreaktionen im Autogenen Training und waehrend der Hypnotherapie. *Zeitschrift fuer Psychologie, 167,* 80–106.

Fray, J. M. (1975). *Implications of electromyographic feedback for Essential Hypertensive patients.* Unpublished doctoral dissertation, Texas Tech University.

Freedman, R. R., & Ianni, P. (1983). Self-control of digital temperature: Physiological factors and transfer effects. *Psychophysiology, 20,* 682–689.

Freedman, R., Ianni, P., & Wenig, P. (1983). Behavioral treatment of Raynaud's disease. *Journal of Consulting and Clinical Psychology, 51,* 539–549.

Green, E. E., Green A. M., Walters, E. D., Sargent, J. D., & Meyer, R. G. (1975). Autogenic feedback training. *Psychotherapy and Psychosomatics, 25,* 88–98.

Haynes, R. B., & Dantes, R. (1987). Patient compliance and the conduct and interpretation of therapeutic trials. *Controlled Clinical Trials, 8,* 12–19.

Haynes, R. B., Taylor, D. W., & Sackett, D. L. (1979). *Compliance in health care.* Baltimore: The Johns Hopkins University Press.

Heide, F. J., & Borkovec, T. D. (1983). Relaxation-induced anxiety: Paradoxical anxiety enhancement due to relaxation training. *Journal of Consulting and Clinical Psychology, 51,* 171–182.

Heide, F. J., & Borkovec, T. D. (1984). Relaxation-induced anxiety: Mechanisms and their theoretical implications. *Behavior Research and Therapy, 22,* 1–12.

Herbert, C. P., & Gutman, G. M. (1983). Practical group autogenic training for management of stress-related disorders in family practice. *Canadian Family Physician, 29*, 109–117.

Hoelscher, T. J., Lichstein, K. L., & Rosenthal, T. L. (1986). Home relaxation practice in hypertension treatment: Objective assessment and compliance induction. *Journal of Consulting and Clinical Psychology, 54*, 217–221.

Hohn, J. M. (1966) *Aenderung der Waermetransportzahl der Haut unter dem Einfluss von durchblutungsfoerdernden Medikamenten und Autogenem Training.* Unpublished doctoral dissertation, Tuebingen University Medical School.

Israel, L., & Rohmer, F. (1958). Variations électroencéphalographiques au cours de la relaxation autogène et hypnotique. In P. Aboulker, L. Chertok, & M. Sapir (Eds.), *La relaxation: Aspects théoriques et pratiques.* Paris: Expansion Scientifique Française.

Jacob, R. G., Kraemer, H. C., & Agras, W. S. (1977). Relaxation therapy in the treatment of hypertension: A review. *Archives of General Psychiatry, 34*, 1417–1427.

Jacobs, G. D., & Lubar, J. F. (1989). Spectral analysis of the central nervous system effects of the relaxation response elicited by autogenic training. *Behavioral Medicine,* 125–132.

Jacobson, E. (1938). *Progressive relaxation.* Chicago: University of Chicago Press.

Jacobson, N. S., Follette, W. L., & Revenstorf, D. (1984). Psychotherapy outcome research: Methods of reporting variability and evaluating clinical significance. *Behavior Therapy, 15*, 336–352.

Janssen, K., & Neutgens, J. (1986). Autogenic training and progressive relaxation in the treatment of three kinds of headache. *Behavior Research and Therapy, 24*, 199–208.

Juenet, C., Cottraux, J., & Collet, L. (1983, December). *GSR feedback and Schultz's relaxation in tension headache: A comparative study.* Paper presented at the 17th Annual Convention of the Association for the Advancement of Behavior Therapy. Washington, D.C.

Jus, A., & Jus, K. (1968). Das Verhalten des Elektroenceophalogramms waehrend des Autogenen Trainings. In D. Langen (Ed.), *Der Weg des Autogenen Trainings* (pp. 359–375). Darmstadt/Germany: Wissenschaftliche Buchgesellschaft.

Kahn, M., Weiss, J. M., & Baker, B. L. (1968). Treatment of insomnia by relaxation training. *Journal of Abnormal Psychology, 73*, 556–558.

Katzenstein, A. (1967). EEG-Untersuchungen unter der Hypnose. *Psychiatrie, Neurologie und Medizinische Psychologie, 19*, 407–410.

Katzenstein, A., Kriegel, E., & Gaefke, I. (1974). Erfolgsuntersuchung bei einer komplexen Psychotherapie essentieller Hypertoniker. *Psychiatrie, Neurologie, Medizinische Psychologie, 26,* 732–737.

Keefe, F. J. (1978). Biofeedback vs. instructional control of skin temperature. *Journal of Behavior Medicine, 1,* 383–390.

Keefe, F. J., Surwit, R. S., & Pilon, R. N. (1979). A 1-year follow-up of Raynaud's patients treated with behavioral therapy techniques. *Journal of Behavioral Medicine, 2,* 385–391.

Keefe, F. J., Surwit, R. S., & Pilon, R. N. (1980). Biofeedback, autogenic training, and progressive relaxation in the treatment of Raynaud's disease. A comparative study. *Journal of Applied Behavior Analysis, 13,* 3–11.

Kelton, A., & Belar, C. D. (1983). The relative efficacy of autogenic phrases and autogenic feedback training in teaching hand warming to children. *Biofeedback and Self-Regulation, 8,* 461–475.

Koldewy, G., & Wegschneider, K. (1963). Autogenes Training bei der Behandlung von Enuretikern. *Zeitschrift fuer Psychotherapie und Medizinsche Psychologie, 13,* 27–31.

Krapf, G. (1984). Erfahrungen mit der Oberstufe des Autogenen Trainings. In G. Iversen (Ed.), *Dem Wegbereiter Johann Heinrich Schultz* (pp. 25–31). Koeln: Deutscher Aerzte Verlag .

Kuhn, T. (1970). *The structure of scientific revolutions* (2nd ed.). Chicago: University of Chicago Press.

Laberke, J. A. (1952). Ueber eine psychosomatische Kombinations—behandlung (mehrdimensionale Therapie) bei sogenannten inneren Krankheiten. *Muenchner Medizinische Wochenschrift, 94,* 1718–1724, 1809–1816.

Lantzsch, W., & Drunkenmoelle, C. (1975). Studien der Durchblutung in Patienten mit Essentieller Hypertonie [Studies of the circulation in patients with Essential Hypertension]. *Psychiatria Clinica, 8,* 223–228.

Lehrer, P. M. & Woolfolk, R. L. (1984). Are stress reduction techniques interchangeable, or do they have specific effects?: A review of the comparative empirical literature. In Woolfook, R. L., & Lehrer, P. M. (Eds.), *Principles and practice of stress management* (pp. 404–477). New York: Guilford Press.

Lehrer, P. M., Woolfolk, R. L., Rooney, A. J., McCann, B., & Carrington, P. (1983). Progressive relaxation and meditation. *Behavior Research and Therapy, 21,* 651–662.

Lichstein, K. L. (1988). *Clinical relaxation strategies.* New York: John Wiley & Sons.

Lindemann, H. (1974). *Ueberleben im Stress: Autogenes Training.* Bertelsmann: Muenchen.

Linden, M. (1977). Verlaufsstudie des Wechsels der Atmung und des CO_2 Spiegels waehrend des Lernens des Autogenen Trainings. *Psychotherapie und Medizinische Psychologie, 27,* 229–234.

Linden, W. (1984). *Psychological perspectives of Essential Hypertension: Etiology, maintenance and treatment.* Basel/New York: S. Karger.

Linden, W. (1987). A microanalysis of autonomic activity during human speech. *Psychosomatic Medicine, 49,* 562–578.

Linden, W. (Ed.). (1988). *Biological barriers in behavioral medicine.* New York: Plenum.

Linden, W., & Frankish, C. J. (1988). Expectancy and type of activity: Effects on pre-stress cardiovascular adaptation. *Biological Psychology, 27,* 227–235.

Linden, W., & Wen, F. (in press). Therapy outcome research, social policy, and the continuing lack of accumulated knowledge. *Professional Psychology: Research and Practice.*

Luborsky, L. Ancona, L., Masoni, A., Scolari, G., & Longoni, A. (1980–1981). Behavioral vs. pharmacological treatments for essential hypertension: A pilot study. *International Journal of Psychiatry in Medicine, 10,* 33–39.

Luiselli, J. K., Steinman, D. L., Marholin, D., II, & Steinman, W. M. (1981). Evaluation of progressive muscle relaxation with conduct-problem, learning-disabled children. *Child Behavior Therapy, 3,* 41–55.

Luthe, W. (1963). Autogenic training: Method, research and application in medicine. *American Journal of Psychotherapy, 17,* 174–195.

Luthe, W., & Schultz, J. H. (1969a). *Autogenic therapy, Vol. II: Medical applications.* New York: Grune & Stratton. (For the reference to Vol. I see Schultz.)

Luthe, W., & Schultz, J. H. (1969b). *Autogenic therapy, Vol. III; Applications in psychotherapy.* New York: Grune & Stratton.

Luthe, W. (1970a). *Autogenic therapy, Vol. IV; Research and theory.* New York: Grune & Stratton.

Luthe, W. (1970b). *Autogenic therapy, Vol. V: Dynamics of autogenic neutralization.* New York: Grune & Stratton.

Luthe, W. (1970c). *Autogenic therapy, Vol. VI; Treatment with autogenic neutralization.* New York: Grune & Stratton.

Martin, A. R. (1951). The fear of relaxation and leisure. *American Journal of Psychoanalysis, 11,* 42–50.

Mensen, H. (1975). *ABC des Autogenen Trainings.* Muenchen: Goldmann.

Miller, N. E. (1969). Learning of visceral and glandular responses. *Science, 163,* 434–445.

Motoda, K., Shibata, J. I., Inanaga, K., & Isozaki, H. (1969). Visual-evoked responses in schizophrenics during autogenic training. *The American Journal of Clinical Hypnosis, 12,* 67–75.

Nicassio, P., & Bootzin, R. (1974). A comparison of progressive relaxation and autogenic training as treatment for insomnia. *Journal of Abnormal Psychology, 83,* 253–260.

Norton, G. R., & Johnson, W. E. (1983). A comparison of two relaxation procedures for reducing cognitive and somatic anxiety. *Journal of Behavior Therapy and Experimental Psychiatry, 14,* 209–214.

Norton, G. R., Rhodes, L., Hauch, J., & Kaprowy, E. A. (1985). Characteristics of subjects experiencing relaxation and relaxation-induced anxiety. *Journal of Behavior Therapy and Experimental Psychiatry, 16,* 211–216.

Ohno, Y. (1965). Studies on physiological effects of autosuggestion centered around autogenic training. *Fukuoka Acta Medica, 56,* 1102–1119.

O'Leary, K. D., & Wilson, G. T. (1987). *Behavior therapy: Application and outcome* (2nd ed.). Englewood Cliffs, NJ: Prentice-Hall.

O'Moore, A. M., O'Moore, R. R., Harrison, R. F., Murphy, G., & Carruthers, M. E. (1983). Psychosomatic aspects in idiopathic infertility: Effects of treatment with autogenic training. *Journal of Psychosomatic Research, 27,* 145–151.

Paul, G. L. (1969). Physiological effects of relaxation training and hypnotic suggestion. *Journal of Abnormal Psychology, 74,* 425–437.

Pelliccioni, R., & Liebner, K. H. (1980). Ultraschall-Doppler sonographische Messungen von Blutstroemungsaenderungen waehrend der Grunduebungen im Rahmen des Autogenen Trainings. *Psychiatrie, Neurologie, und Medizinische Psychologie, 32,* 290–297.

Perloff, D., Sokolow, M., & Cowan, R. (1983). The prognostic value of ambulatory blood pressure. *Journal of the American Medical Association, 249,* 2792–2798.

Pikoff, H. (1984). A critical review of autogenic training in America. *Clinical Psychology Review, 4,* 619–639.

Polacková, J., Bocková, E., & Sedivec, V. (1982). Autogenic training: Application in secondary prevention of myocardial infarction. *Activitas Nervosa Superior, 24,* 178–180.

Polzien, P. (1953). Versuche zur Normalisierung der S-T Strecke und T-zacke im EKG von der Psyche her. *Zeitschrift fuer Kreislauf-Forschung, 42,* 9–10.

Polzien, P. (1955). Die Aenderung der Temperaturregulation bei der Gesamtumschaltung durch das Autogene Training. Ein physikalischer Nachweis des hypnotischen Zustandes. *Zeitschrift fuer Experimentelle Medizin, 125,* 469–481.

Prill, H. J. (1965). Das Autogene Training in der Geburtschilfe und Gynaekologie. In W. Luthe (Ed.), *Autogenes Training: Correlationes psychosomaticae* (pp. 234–246). Stuttgart, FRG: G. Thieme Verlag.

Raimy, V. (1975). *Misunderstandings of the self.* San Francisco: Jossey-Bass.

Reed, R., & Meyer, R. G. (1974). Reduction of test anxiety via autogenic therapy. *Psychological Reports, 35,* 649–650.

Rossi, N., Caldari, R., Costa, F. V., & Ambrosioni, E. (1989). Autogenic training in mild essential hypertension: A placebo-controlled study. *Stress Medicine, 5,* 63–68.

Sakakura, Y., Iwabuchi, S., & Murata, T. (1967). Psychosomatic studies on infertility due to tubal factors. In Abstracts and papers, *International Congress for Psychosomatic Medicine and Hypnosis* (p. 121), Kyoto, Japan.

Sapir, M., & Reverchon, F. (1965). Modifications objectives circulatoires et digestives au cours du Training Autogène. In W. Luthe (Ed.), *Autogenes Training; Correlationes psychosomaticae* (pp. 59–63). Stuttgart: Thieme.

Sargent, J. D., Greene, E. E., & Walters, E. D. (1973). Preliminary report on the use of autogenic feedback training on the treatment of migraine and tension headaches. *Psychosomatic Medicine, 35,* 129–135.

Sargent, J., Solbach, P., Coyne, L., Spohn, H., & Segerson, J. (1986). Results of a controlled, experimental, outcome study of nondrug treatments for the control of migraine headaches. *Journal of Behavioral Medicine, 9,* 291–323.

Scallet, A., Cloniger, C. R., & Othmer, E. (1976). The management of chronic hysteria: A review and double-blind trial of electro-sleep and other relaxation methods. *Diseases of the Nervous System, 37,* 347–353.

Schaefgen, E. (1984). Lebensweg von J. H. Schultz nach seinem "Lebensbilderbuch eines Nervenarztes." In G. Iversen (Ed.), *Dem Wegbereiter Johann Heinrich Schultz* (pp. 57–60). Koeln: Deutscher Aerzte Verlag.

Schultz, J. H. (1973). *Das Autogene Training-Konzentrative Selbstentspannung. Versuch einer Klinisch-praktischen Darstellung.* Stuttgart, FRG: G. Thieme Verlag.

Schultz, J. H., & Luthe, W. (1969). *Autogenic therapy, Vol. I: Autogenic Methods.* New York: Grune & Stratton.

Schultz, J. H. (1932). *Das Autogene Training (Konzentrative Selbstentspannung).* Leipzig: Thieme.

Schwartz, G. E. (1977). Psychosomatic disorders and biofeedback: A psychological model of disregulation. In J. D. Maser & M. E. P. Seligman (Eds.), *Psychopathology; Experimental models* (pp. 270–307). San Francisco: Freeman.

Schwartz, G. E., Davidson, R. J., & Goleman, D. J. (1978). Patterning of cognitive and somatic processes in the self-regulation of anxiety: Effects of meditation versus exercise. *Psychosomatic Medicine, 40,* 321–328.

Schwarz, G., & Langen, D. (1966). Gefaessreaktionen bei Autogenem Training und niedrigen Raumtemperaturen. In J. J. Lopez Ibor (Ed.), *IV World Congress of Psychiatry, Madrid* (International Congress Series, No. 117). Amsterdam: Excerpta Medica Foundation.

Schwartz, M. S., & Associates. (1987). *Biofeedback: A practitioner's guide.* New York: Guilford Press.

Sellers, D. J. (1974). Teaching a self-initiated control technique to individuals and a group in college. *The International Journal of Clinical and Experimental Hypnosis, 22,* 39–45.

Selye, H. (1956). *The stress of life.* New York: McGraw-Hill.

Shapiro, S., & Lehrer, P. M. (1980). Psychophysiological effects of autogenic training and progressive relaxation. *Biofeedback and Self-Regulation, 5,* 249–255.

Shapiro, D. A., & Shapiro, D. (1982). Meta-analysis of comparative therapy outcome studies: A replication and refinement. *Psychological Bulletin, 92,* 581–604.

Siebenthal, W. von. (1952). Eine vereinfachte Schwereuebung des Schultz'schen Autogenen Trainings. *Zeitschrift fuer Psychotherapie und Medizinische Psychologie, 2,* 135–143.

Sipos, K. Bodo, M., Nagypal, T., & Tomka, I. (1978). Analysis of EEG during autogenic training. *Activitas Nervosa Superior, 20,* 95–96.

Spiess, K., Sachs, G., Buchinger, C., Roleggla, G., Schmack, C., & Haber, P. (1988). Zur Auswirkung von Informations—und Entspannungsgruppen auf die Lungenfunktion und psychophysische Befindlichkeit bei Asthmapatienten. *Praxis der Klinischen Pneumologie, 42,* 641–644.

Surwit, R. S., Pilon, R. N., & Fenton, C. H. (1978). Behavioral treatment of Raynaud's disease. *Journal of Behavioral Medicine, 1,* 323–335.

Taylor, C. B., Agras, W. S., Schneider, J. A., & Allen, R. A. (1983). Adherence to instructions to practice relaxation exercises. *Journal of Consulting and Clinical Psychology, 51,* 952–953.

Tebecis, A. K., Ohno, Y., Matsubara, H., Sugano, H., Takeya, T., Ikemi, Y., & Takasaki, M. (1976/77). A longitudinal study of some physiological parameters and autogenic training. *Psychotherapy and Psychosomatics, 27,* 8–17.

Tebecis, A. K., Ohno, Y., Takeya, T., Sugano, H., Matsubara, H., Tanaka, Y., Ikemi, Y., & Takasaki, M. (1977). Fine body movement during autogenic training. *Biofeedback and Self-regulation, 2,* 417–427.

Toscano, W. B., & Cowings, P. S. (1982). Reducing motion sickness: A comparison of autogenic-feedback training and an alternative cognitive task. *Aviation, Space, and Environmental Medicine, 53,* 449–453.

Vinck, J., Arickx, M., & Honenaert, M. (1987). Predicting interindividual differences in blood pressure response to relaxation training in normotensives. *Journal of Behavioral Medicine, 10,* 395–410.

Wallace, R. K. (1970). Physiological effects of transcendental meditation. *Science, 167,* 1751–1754.

Wallace, R. K., & Benson, H. (1972). The physiology of meditation. *Scientific American, 226,* 84–90.

Woolfolk, R. L., & Lehrer, P. M. (Eds.). (1984). *Principles and practice of stress management.* New York: Guilford Press.

Woolfolk, R. L., Lehrer, P. M., McCann, B. S., & Rooney, A. (1982). Effects of progressive relaxation and meditation on cognitive and somatic manifestations of daily stress. *Behaviour Research and Therapy, 20,* 461–468.

Zimmermann-Tansella, C., Dolcetta, G., Azzini, V., Zacche, G., Bertagnio, P., Siani, R., & Tansella, M. (1979). Preparation courses for childbirth in primipara: A comparison. *Journal of Psychosomatic Research, 23,* 227–233.

Appendix

This appendix provides an example of the AT rationale (given in session 1), a suggested outline for an autogenic training program of eight weekly sessions, and a sample diary page for the trainees to use. Only the core ideas of the rationale are included. The appendix serves as a quick reference for AT therapists who have familiarized themselves with the content of the book and only require an outline for the standardization of their autogenics teachings.

Sample Rationale

Autogenic training is a systematic teaching program that will help you learn to relax your body and is especially useful in periods of stress to help you return to a balanced, normal state. It is one of the most effective and comprehensive reducers of chronic stress, and has been used for over 50 years with considerable success.

When you do not have time to recover from emotionally and physically stressful events, a number of disturbances within your body's physiology are likely to occur and you may experience feelings of fatigue, tension, and anxiety, which may then contribute to a variety of psychosomatic problems like ulcers, migraines, and tension headaches, or it may aggravate arthritis or contribute to high blood pressure. Autogenic training is a self-hypnotic procedure, which means that nobody is doing anything *to* you. It is my intention as a trainer of autogenics to teach you how to do it yourself so that you can train and later on apply autogenics anytime you want and anywhere you want without extra help. This is the great advantage of a method of this type because it is relatively quick and easy to learn, and it becomes a permanent part of your repertoire of stress coping skills that you are unlikely to forget and that you can practice when and where you want.

Learning to relax with or without the use of autogenic training is a natural skill, but many adults have forgotten how to use it. You can best observe this when you watch small children or pets. When children or pets are deeply asleep you can lift any of their limbs, and when you let it loose, it will fall heavily to the ground because there is no muscle tension. Neither the sleeping child nor the animal will show an alarm response to your having lifted the limb. However, when you try this with an adult you will find that the arm will stay up or go down quite slowly because they never really seem to fully relax their muscles. As with any other skill it is important for you to face the fact that skills need learning and practice. Therefore, it is very important that you follow the instructions for practice that you'll be given and that you work hard at setting up an optimal training program because just like becoming a good baseball pitcher or a tennis player, or just like a child learning to walk or to talk, AT needs practice and practice and refinement and refinement if you want to really learn it well.

You may wonder how autogenic training will help you relax. The method is actually quite simple. You will learn six formulas, which you will say to yourself and for which you will try to develop images. These images are most effective when they mean something to you. The six formulas of AT refer to very particular body functions that you would like to regulate and relax. The first formula refers to heaviness in the limbs, and the second formula deals with feelings of warmth. Both the heaviness and warmth sensations have been demonstrated to be associated with regular and even blood flow in your limbs and reduced muscle tone. By developing these images and practicing concentration on these images, you will actually learn to achieve this just as have thousands of people before you. The third formula will concentrate on your heart and has the effect of regulating and calming your heart activity. The fourth formula refers to respiration and serves to calm and even out your breathing. The fifth exercise will relax and warm your abdominal region and have positive effects on all your inner organs, and the sixth and last formula will reduce the flow of blood to your head and will help you to achieve good head relaxation. I will teach you these formulas in a step-by-step procedure that is going to last a total of 8 weeks. In the sessions we will talk about the sensations you have experienced, the progress you have made, and the difficulties that you have had in achieving progress. I strongly expect that you will have learned autogenics by the eighth week and will have had little difficulty in becoming aware of these sensations.

Suggested Program Outline

Session 1

Objectives: Explain the rationale, body positions, taking back procedure, desirable and possibly undesirable effects, and the home practice of autogenics.

The complete instructions for exercise 1 are:

"Close your eyes, find a comfortable position, and allow yourself to concentrate on what is going on inside of you. Nobody will disturb you. Just relax a while." (*2 minutes*)

"Now concentrate on your dominant arm and repeat the formula six times, slowly. Use an image of heaviness that makes sense to you. The formula is: 'My right (left) arm is very heavy.' Use the formula six times." (*1 minute*)

"Now turn your attention away from the dominant arm and say to yourself, just once: 'I am very quiet,' and enjoy feeling relaxed for a while." (*2 minutes*)

"Now concentrate on your dominant arm again and repeat the formula six times, slowly. Use an image of heaviness that makes sense to you. The formula is: 'My right (left) arm is very heavy.' Use the formula six times." (*1 minute*)

(cont.)

"Now direct your attention away from the dominant arm again, and say to yourself, just once: 'I am very quiet,' and enjoy feeling relaxed for a while." (*2 minutes*)

"I will soon ask you to take back, counting down from four to one." (*Wait 15 seconds, then start counting down.*) "Four, make a couple of fists in rapid succession to get the blood pumping again." (*Wait 15 seconds.*) "Three, bend your arms inward a few times." (*Wait 15 seconds.*) "Two, take a few deep breaths and fill your lungs with air." (*Wait 15 seconds.*) "And, one, open your eyes, sit up, and you feel relaxed yet alert."

Total time: 9 minutes

Session 2

Objective: Review past practice experience and train new warmth formula.

The complete instructions for adding formula 2 are:

"Close your eyes, find a comfortable position, and allow yourself to concentrate on what is going on inside of you. Nobody will disturb you. Just relax for a while." (*2 minutes*)

"Now concentrate on your dominant arm and repeat the formula six times, slowly. Use an image of heaviness that makes sense to you. The formula is: 'My right (left) arm is very heavy.' Use the formula six times." (*1 minute*)

"Now turn your attention away from the dominant arm and say to yourself, just once: 'I am very quiet,' and enjoy feeling relaxed for a while." (*2 minutes*)

"Now concentrate on your dominant arm again and repeat the formula six times, slowly. Use an image of heaviness that makes sense to you. The formula is: 'My right (left) arm is very heavy.' Use the formula six times." (*1 minute*)

"Now direct your attention away from the dominant arm
(cont.)

again, and say to yourself, just once: 'I am very quiet,' and enjoy feeling relaxed for a while." (*2 minutes*)

"I will soon ask you to take back, counting down from four to one." (*Wait 15 seconds, then start counting down.*) "Four, make a couple of fists in rapid succession to get the blood pumping again." (*Wait 15 seconds.*) "Three, bend your arms inward a few times." (*Wait 15 seconds.*) "Two, take a few deep breaths and fill your lungs with air." (*Wait 15 seconds.*) "And, one, open your eyes, sit up, and you feel relaxed yet alert."

Total time: 9 minutes

Session 3

Objectives: Review home practice and train new combined heaviness and warmth formula.

The complete instructions for combining formulas 1 and 2 are:

"Close your eyes, find a comfortable position, and allow yourself to concentrate on what is going on inside of you. Nobody will disturb you. Just relax for a while." (*2 minutes*)

"Now concentrate on both arms and repeat the formula six times, slowly. Use an image of heaviness that makes sense to you. The formula is: 'My arms are very heavy and warm.' Use the formula six times." (*1 minute*)

"Now turn your attention away from the arms and say to yourself, just once: 'I am very quiet,' and enjoy feeling relaxed for a while." (*2 minutes*)

"Now concentrate on your arms again and repeat the formula ('My arms are very heavy and warm.') six times, slowly. Use an image of warmth and heaviness that makes sense to you. Use the formula six times." (*1 minute*)

(cont.)

"Now direct your attention away from the arms again, and say to yourself, just once: 'I am very quiet,' and enjoy feeling relaxed for a while." (*2 minutes*)

"I will soon ask you to take back, counting down from four to one." (*Wait 15 seconds, then start counting down.*) "Four, make a couple of fists in rapid succession to get the blood pumping again." (*Wait 15 seconds.*) "Three, bend your arms inward a few times." (*Wait 15 seconds.*) "Two, take a few deep breaths and fill your lungs with air." (*Wait 15 seconds.*) "And, one, open your eyes, sit up, and you feel relaxed yet alert."

Total time: 9 minutes

Session 4

Objective: Review home practice and train new formula for heart regulation.

The complete instructions for adding formula 3 are:

"Close your eyes, find a comfortable position, and allow yourself to concentrate on what is going on inside of you. Nobody will disturb you. Just relax for a while." (*2 minutes*)

"Now concentrate on both arms and repeat the formula six times, slowly. Use an image of heaviness that makes sense to you. The formula is: 'My arms are very heavy and warm.' Use the formula six times." (*1 minute*)

"Now turn your attention away from the arms and say to yourself, just once: 'I am very quiet,' and enjoy feeling relaxed for a while." (*2 minutes*)

"Now concentrate on the beating of your heart, and repeat the formula ('My heartbeat is calm and strong.') six times, slowly. Use the formula six times." (*1 minute*)

"Now direct your attention away from the heart and say to
(cont.)

yourself, just once: 'I am very quiet,' and enjoy feeling relaxed for a while." (*2 minutes*)

"I will soon ask you to take back, counting down from four to one." (*Wait 15 seconds, then start counting down.*) "Four, make a couple of fists in rapid succession to get the blood pumping again." (*Wait 15 seconds.*) "Three, bend your arms inward a few times." (*Wait 15 seconds.*) "Two, take a few deep breaths and fill your lungs with air." (*Wait 15 seconds.*) "And, one, open your eyes, sit up, and you feel relaxed yet alert."

Total time: 9 minutes

Session 5

Objective: Review home practice and train new breathing formula.

The complete instructions for adding formula 4 are:

"Close your eyes, find a comfortable position, and allow yourself to concentrate on what is going on inside of you. Nobody will disturb you. Just relax for a while." (*2 minutes*)

"Now concentrate on both arms and repeat the formula six times, slowly. Use an image of heaviness that makes sense to you. The formula is: 'My arms are very heavy and warm.' Use the formula six times." (*1 minute*)

"Now turn your attention away from the arms and say to yourself, just once: 'I am very quiet,' and enjoy feeling relaxed for a while." (*2 minutes*)

"Now concentrate on the beating of your heart, and repeat the formula ('My heartbeat is calm and strong.') six times, slowly. Use the formula six times." (*1 minute*)

"Now direct your attention away from the heart and say to yourself, just once: 'I am very quiet,' and enjoy feeling relaxed for a while." (*2 minutes*)

(cont.)

"Now concentrate on the rhythm of your breathing and repeat the formula ('It breathes me.') six times, slowly." (*1 minute*)

"Now direct your attention away from the breathing and say to yourself, just once: 'I am very quiet,' and enjoy feeling relaxed for a while." (*2 minutes*)

"I will soon ask you to take back, counting down from four to one." (*Wait 15 seconds, then start counting down.*) "Four, make a couple of fists in rapid succession to get the blood pumping again." (*Wait 15 seconds.*) "Three, bend your arms inward a few times." (*Wait 15 seconds.*) "Two, take a few deep breaths and fill your lungs with air." (*Wait 15 seconds.*) "And, one, open your eyes, sit up, and you feel relaxed yet alert."

Total time: 12 minutes

Session 6

Objective: Review home practice and train solar plexus exercise.

The complete instructions for adding formula 5 are:

"Close your eyes, find a comfortable position, and allow yourself to concentrate on what is going on inside of you. Nobody will disturb you. Just relax for a while." (*2 minutes*)

"Now concentrate on both arms and repeat the formula six times, slowly. Use an image of heaviness that makes sense to you. The formula is: 'My arms are very heavy and warm.' Use the formula six times." (*1 minute*)

"Now turn your attention away from the arms and say to yourself, just once: 'I am very quiet,' and enjoy feeling relaxed for a while." (*2 minutes*)

"Now concentrate on the beating of your heart, and repeat
(cont.)

the formula ('My heartbeat is calm and strong.') six times, slowly (*1 minute*).

"Now direct your attention away from the heart and say to yourself, just once: 'I am very quiet,' and enjoy feeling relaxed for a while." (*1 minute*)

"Now concentrate on the rhythm of your breathing and repeat the formula ('It breathes me.') six times, slowly." (*1 minute*)

"Now direct your attention away from the breathing and say to yourself, just once: 'I am very quiet,' and enjoy feeling relaxed for a while." (*2 minutes*)

"Now concentrate on your stomach area and repeat the formula ('Warmth is radiating over my stomach.') six times, slowly." (*1 minute*)

"Now direct your attention away from the stomach area and say to yourself, just once: 'I am very quiet,' and enjoy feeling relaxed for a while." (*2 minutes*)

"I will soon ask you to take back, counting down from four to one." (*Wait 15 seconds, then start counting down.*) "Four, make a couple of fists in rapid succession to get the blood pumping again." (*Wait 15 seconds.*) "Three, bend your arms inward a few times." (*Wait 15 seconds.*) "Two, take a few deep breaths and fill your lungs with air." (*Wait 15 seconds.*) "And, one, open your eyes, sit up, and you feel relaxed yet alert."

Total time: 15 minutes

Session 7

Objective: Review home practice and train forehead exercise.
The complete instructions for adding formula 6 are:

"Close your eyes, find a comfortable position, and allow yourself to concentrate on what is going on inside of you. No

(cont.)

body will disturb you. Just relax for a while." (*2 minutes*)

"Now concentrate on both arms and repeat the formula six times, slowly. Use an image of heaviness that makes sense to you. The formula is: 'My arms are very heavy and warm.' Use the formula six times." (*1 minute*)

"Now turn your attention away from the arms and say to yourself, just once: 'I am very quiet,' and enjoy feeling relaxed for a while." (*1 minute*)

"Now concentrate on the beating of your heart, and repeat the formula ('My heartbeat is calm and strong.') six times, slowly. Use the formula six times." (*1 minute*)

"Now direct your attention away from the heart and say to yourself, just once: 'I am very quiet,' and enjoy feeling relaxed for a while." (*1 minute*)

"Now concentrate on the rhythm of your breathing and repeat the formula ('It breathes me.') six times, slowly." (*1 minute*)

"Now direct your attention away from the breathing and say to yourself, just once: 'I am very quiet,' and enjoy feeling relaxed for a while." (*1 minute*)

"Now concentrate on your stomach area and repeat the formula ('Warmth is radiating over my stomach.') six times, slowly." (*1 minute*)

"Now direct your attention away from the stomach area and say to yourself, just once: 'I am very quiet,' and enjoy feeling relaxed for a while." (*1 minute*)

"Now concentrate on your forehead and repeat the formula ('The forehead is cool.') six times, slowly." (*1 minute*)

"Now direct your attention away from the forehead and say to youself, just once: 'I am very quiet,' and enjoy feeling relaxed for a while." (*2 minutes*)

"I will soon ask you to take back, counting down from four to one." (*Wait 15 seconds, then start counting down.*) "Four, make a couple of fists in rapid succession to get the blood pumping again" (*Wait 15 seconds.*) "Three, bend your arms inward a few

(cont.)

times." (*Wait 15 seconds.*) "Two, take a few deep breaths and fill your lungs with air." (*Wait 15 seconds.*) "And, one, open your eyes, sit up, and you feel relaxed yet alert."

Total time: 14 minutes

Session 8

Objective: Prepare the trainee to use autogenic training independently, give an overall summary evaluation of their training success and difficulties, provide examples where they have already used autogenic training effectively, and highlight situations where they think they will use it in the future. Participants may also express at this time whether they have particular difficulties with the autogenic formulas and discuss with the trainer whether, and if so how, they would want to change the standard formulas to better suit their own needs. Otherwise, formulas remain unchanged from the seventh session.

Sample Diary Page

Training Week:_____ From:_____ To:_____
Training goal for this week: _____

Please tick off (✔) each exercise after you did it and use the following scale to evaluate each time whether or not you reached this week's goal.

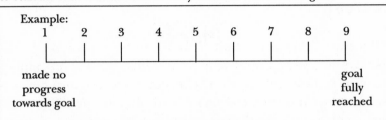

In this example, a "6" is circled and would indicate that you made good progress but still fall short of reaching your goal.

Day 1   Excercise I:_____   Rating:_____ (Fill in appropriate number.)
          Excercies II:_____   Rating:_____
Day 2   Excercise I:_____   Rating:_____
          Excercise II:_____   Rating:_____
Day 3   Excercise I:_____   Rating:_____
          Excercise II:_____   Rating:_____
Day 4   Excercise I:_____   Rating:_____
          Excercise II:_____   Rating:_____
Day 5   Excercise I:_____   Rating:_____
          Excercies II:_____   Rating:_____
Day 6   Excercise I:_____   Rating:_____
          Excercise II:_____   Rating:_____
Day 7   Excercise I:_____   Rating:_____
          Excercise II:_____   Rating:_____

Index